Teach & Test

Math Grade 2

D1611793

Table of Contents

Introduction 2
Stage a Test 2
Helping Hand Test Strategies 3
Constructed-Response Questions 3
Evaluating the Tests 3
Record Sheet 4
Unit 1: Numeration Part I 5
Unit 1 Test 14
Unit 2: Numeration Part II 19
Unit 2 Test 29
Unit 3: Geometry 34
Unit 3 Test 42
Unit 4: Addition Computation 47
Unit 4 Test 58
Midway Review Test 62
Unit 5: Subtraction Computation 67
Unit 5 Test 77
Unit 6: Measurement 81
Unit 6 Test 90
Unit 7: Statistics, Fractions 95
Unit 7 Test 103
Unit 8: Problem Solving 107
Unit 8 Test 114
Final Review Test 119
Answer Key 126
Cross-Reference Guide ..... inside back cover

How to Use This Book

1. This book can be used in a home or classroom setting. Read through each unit before working with the student(s). Familiarize yourself with the vocabulary and the skills that are introduced at the top of each unit activity page. Use this information as a guide to help instruct the student(s).
2. Choose a quiet place with little or no interruptions (including the telephone). Talk with the student(s) about the purpose of this book and how you will be working as a team to prepare for standardized tests.
3. As an option, copy the unit test and give it as a pretest to identify weak areas.
4. Upon the completion of each unit, you will find a unit test. Discuss the Helping Hand strategy for test taking featured on the test. Use the example on each test as a chance to show the student(s) how to work through a problem and completely fill in the answer circle. Encourage the student(s) to work independently when possible, but this is a learning time, and questions should be welcomed. A time limit is given for each test. Instruct the student(s) to use the time allowed efficiently, looking back over the answers if possible. Tell him to continue until he sees the stop sign.
5. Record the score on the record sheet on page 4. If a student has difficulty with any questions, use the cross-reference guide on the inside back cover to identify the skills that need to be reviewed.

Teach & Test

Introduction

Now this makes sense—teaching students the skills and strategies that are expected of them before they are tested!

Many students, parents, and teachers are concerned that standardized test scores do not adequately reflect a child's capabilities. This may be due to one or more of the factors italicized below. The purpose of this book is to reduce the negative impact of these, or similar factors, on a student's standardized test scores. The goal is to target those factors and alter their effects as described.

1. *The student has been taught the tested skills but has forgotten them.* This book is divided into units that are organized similarly to second grade textbooks. Instructions for the skill itself are found at the top of each unit activity page, ensuring that the student has been exposed to each key component. The exercises include drill/practice and creative learning activities. Additional activity suggestions can be found in a star burst within the units. These activities require the students to apply the skills that they are practicing.
2. *The student has mastered the skills but has never seen them presented in a test-type format.* Ideally, the skills a student learns at school will be used as part of problem solving in the outside world. For this reason, the skills in this book, and in most classrooms, are not practiced in a test-type format. At the end of each unit in this book, the skills are specifically matched with test questions. In this way, the book serves as a type of "bridge" between the skills that the student(s) has mastered and the standardized test format.
3. *The student is inexperienced with the answer sheet format.* Depending on the standardized test that your school district uses, students are expected to fill in the answer circles completely and neatly. The unit, midway review, and final review tests will help prepare the student(s) for this process.
4. *The student may feel the anxiety of a new and unfamiliar situation.* While testing, students will notice changes in their daily routine: their classroom door will be closed with a "Testing" sign on it, they will be asked not to use the restroom, their desks may be separated, their teacher may read from a script and refuse to repeat herself, etc. To help relieve the stress caused by these changes, treat each unit test in this book as it would be treated at school by following the procedures listed below.

Stage a Test

You will find review tests midway through the book and again at the end of the book. When you reach these points, "stage a test" by creating a real test-taking environment. The procedures listed below coincide with many standardized test directions. The purpose is to alleviate stress, rather than contribute to it, so make this a serious, but calm, event and the student(s) will benefit.

1. Prepare! Have the student(s) sharpen two pencils, lay out scratch paper, and use the restroom.
2. Choose a room with a door that can be closed. Ask a student to put a sign on the door that reads "Testing" and explain that no talking will be permitted after the sign is hung.
3. Direct the student(s) to turn to a specific page but not to begin until the instructions are completely given.
4. Read the instructions at the top of the page and work through the example together. Discuss the Helping Hand strategy that is featured at the top of the page. Have the student(s) neatly and completely fill in the bubble for the example. This is the child's last chance to ask for help!
5. Instruct the student(s) to continue working until the stop sign is reached. If a student needs help reading, you may read each question only once.

Helping Hand Test Strategies

The first page of each test features a specific test-taking strategy that will be helpful in working through most standardized tests. These strategies are introduced and spotlighted one at a time so that they will be learned and remembered internally. Each will serve as a valuable test-taking tool, so discuss them thoroughly.

The strategies include:

- Read all of the choices before you answer.
- Cross out answers you know are wrong.
- Sometimes looking at all of the choices gets confusing. Cover three answers and look at each one separately.
- Find your own answer before you look at the choices.
- When using scratch paper, copy carefully.
- Use your time wisely. If a problem seems tough, skip it and come back to it later.
- Compare the answer choices. Some answer choices may look very similar.
- Always read the question twice. Does your answer make sense?

Constructed-Response Questions

You will find the final question of each test is written in a different format called constructed response. This means that students are not provided with answer choices, but are instead asked to construct their own answers. The objective of such an "open-ended" type of question is to provide students with a chance to creatively develop reasonable answers. It also provides an insight to a student's reasoning and thinking skills. As this format is becoming more accepted and encouraged by standardized test developers, students will be "ahead of the game" by practicing such responses now.

Evaluating the Tests

Two types of questions are included in each test. The unit tests and the midway review test each consist of 20 multiple-choice questions, and the final review test consists of 30 multiple-choice questions. All tests include a constructed response question which requires the student(s) to construct and sometimes support an answer. Use the following procedures to evaluate a student's performance on each test.

1. Use the answer key found on pages 126–128 to correct the tests. Be sure the student(s) neatly and completely filled in the answer circles.
2. Record the scores on the record sheet found on page 4. If the student(s) incorrectly answered any questions, use the cross-reference guide found on the inside back cover to help identify the skills the student(s) needs to review. Each test question references the corresponding activity page.
3. Scoring the constructed-response questions is somewhat subjective. Discuss these questions with the student(s). Sometimes it is easier for the student(s) to explain the answer verbally. Help the student to record her thoughts as a written answer. If the student(s) has difficulty formulating a response, refer back to the activity pages using the cross-reference guide. Also review the star burst activity found in the unit which also requires the student(s) to formulate an answer.
4. Discuss the test with the student(s). What strategies were used to answer the questions? Were some questions more difficult than others? Was there enough time? What strategies did the student(s) use while taking the test?

Record Sheet

Record a student's score for each test by drawing a star or placing a sticker below each item number that was correct. Leave the incorrect boxes empty as this will allow you to visually see any weak spots. Review and practice those missed skills, then retest only the necessary items.

Unit 1	1	2	3	4	5	6	7	8	9	10	11	12	13	14	15	16	17	18	19	20

Unit 2	1	2	3	4	5	6	7	8	9	10	11	12	13	14	15	16	17	18	19	20

Unit 3	1	2	3	4	5	6	7	8	9	10	11	12	13	14	15	16	17	18	19	20

Unit 4	1	2	3	4	5	6	7	8	9	10	11	12	13	14	15	16	17	18	19	20

Unit 5	1	2	3	4	5	6	7	8	9	10	11	12	13	14	15	16	17	18	19	20

Midway Review Test	1	2	3	4	5	6	7	8	9	10	11	12	13	14	15	16	17	18	19	20

Unit 6	1	2	3	4	5	6	7	8	9	10	11	12	13	14	15	16	17	18	19	20

Unit 7	1	2	3	4	5	6	7	8	9	10	11	12	13	14	15	16	17	18	19	20

Unit 8	1	2	3	4	5	6	7	8	9	10	11	12	13	14	15	16	17	18	19	20

Final Review Test	1	2	3	4	5	6	7	8	9	10	11	12	13	14	15	16	17	18	19	20

21	22	23	24	25	26	27	28	29	30

Name

Groups of tens and ones

Unit 1

What is different about the numbers 9 and 10? The number 9 (1-digit number) only has a digit in the ones place, while the number 10 (2-digit number) has a number in the tens place and the ones place.

Circle the groups of tens. Then write the number two ways as shown.

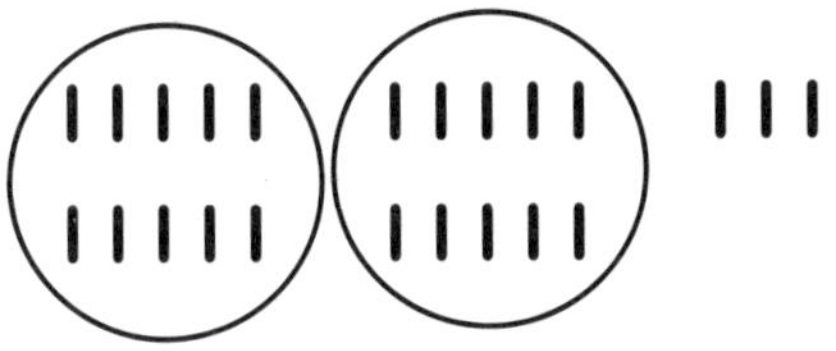

tens	ones
2	3

23

A.

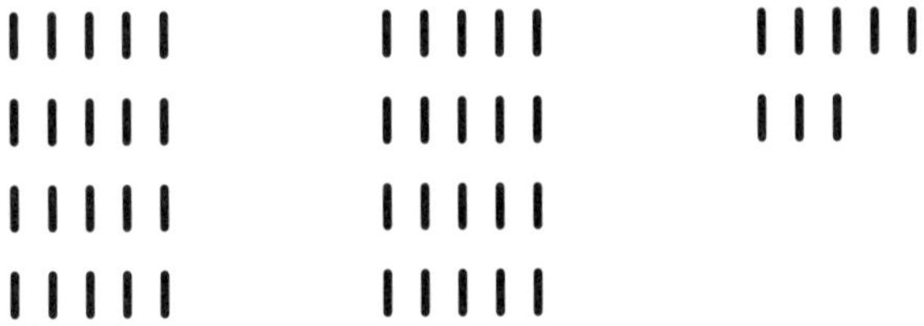

tens	ones

_____

B.

tens	ones

_____

C.

tens	ones

_____

D.

tens	ones

_____

E.

tens	ones

_____

Name

2-digit numbers in expanded notation

Unit 1

Any 2-digit number can be written as an addition problem by separating the tens and ones. This is called **expanded notation**.

Write an addition problem for each picture as shown. Then write the number.

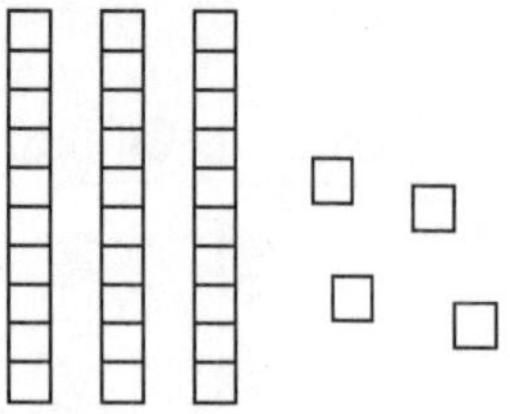

30 + 4 = 34

A. 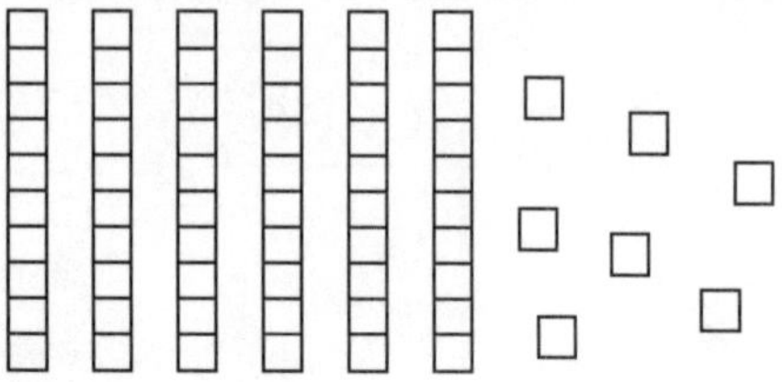

_____ + _____ = _____

B. 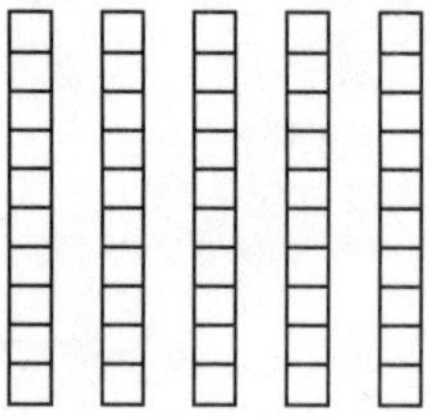

_____ + _____ = _____

C. 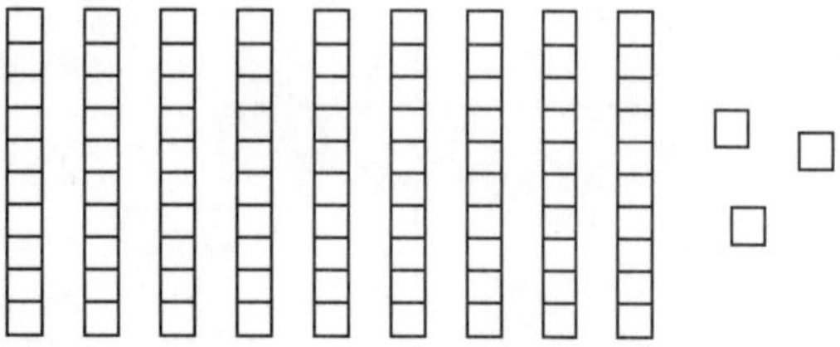

_____ + _____ = _____

D. 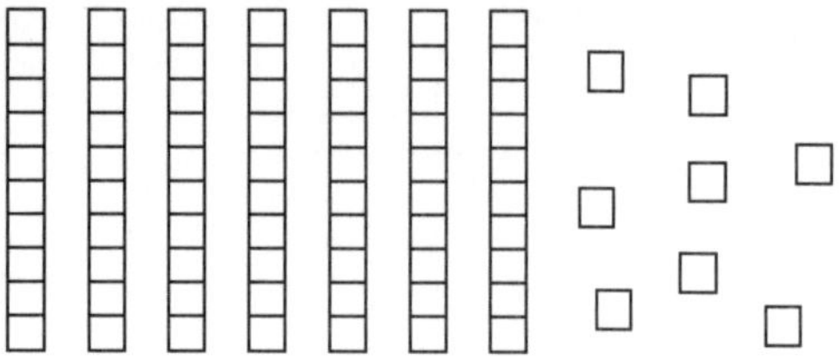

_____ + _____ = _____

Show two other ways to write 41.

Name

2-digit number names

Unit 1

Numbers can be written in word form as well as numerals.
Example: thirty-nine, 39

Color the corresponding space for each number as you read its name. The winner is the first car to reach the flag.

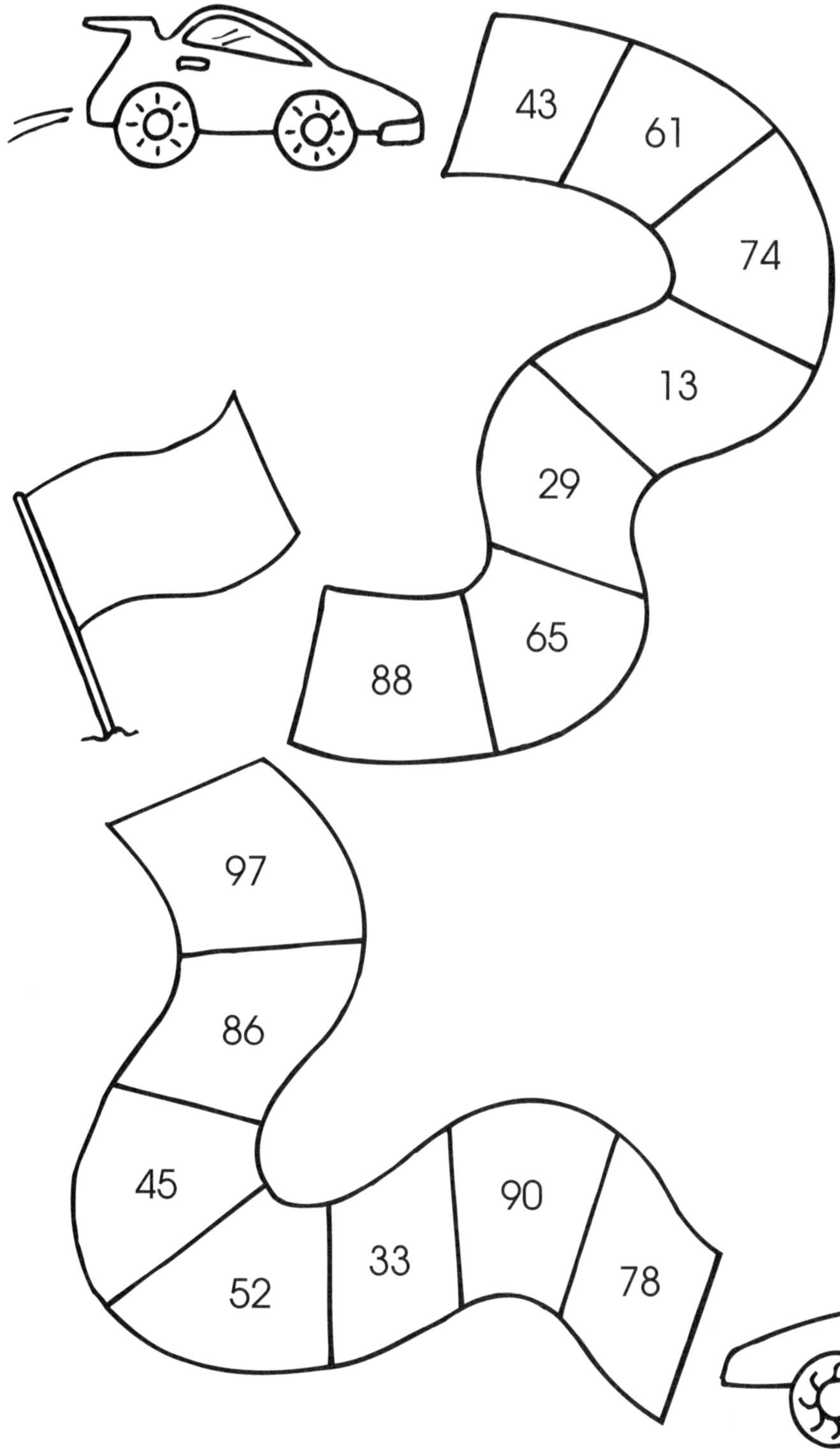

1. forty-three
2. sixty-one
3. seventy-eight
4. seventy-four
5. ninety
6. thirty-three
7. thirteen
8. fifty-two
9. forty-five
10. twenty-nine
11. eighty-six
12. sixty-five
13. ninety-seven

Name

Ordering numbers to 100 — Unit 1

You can order numbers from 1 to 100 by first looking at the tens place and then looking at the ones place. When you reach 100, you will need to look first at the hundreds place.

Cut out the puzzle pieces. Arrange them in a square that will put them in order from 1 to 100. Glue the pieces to another sheet of paper. Fill in the missing numbers.

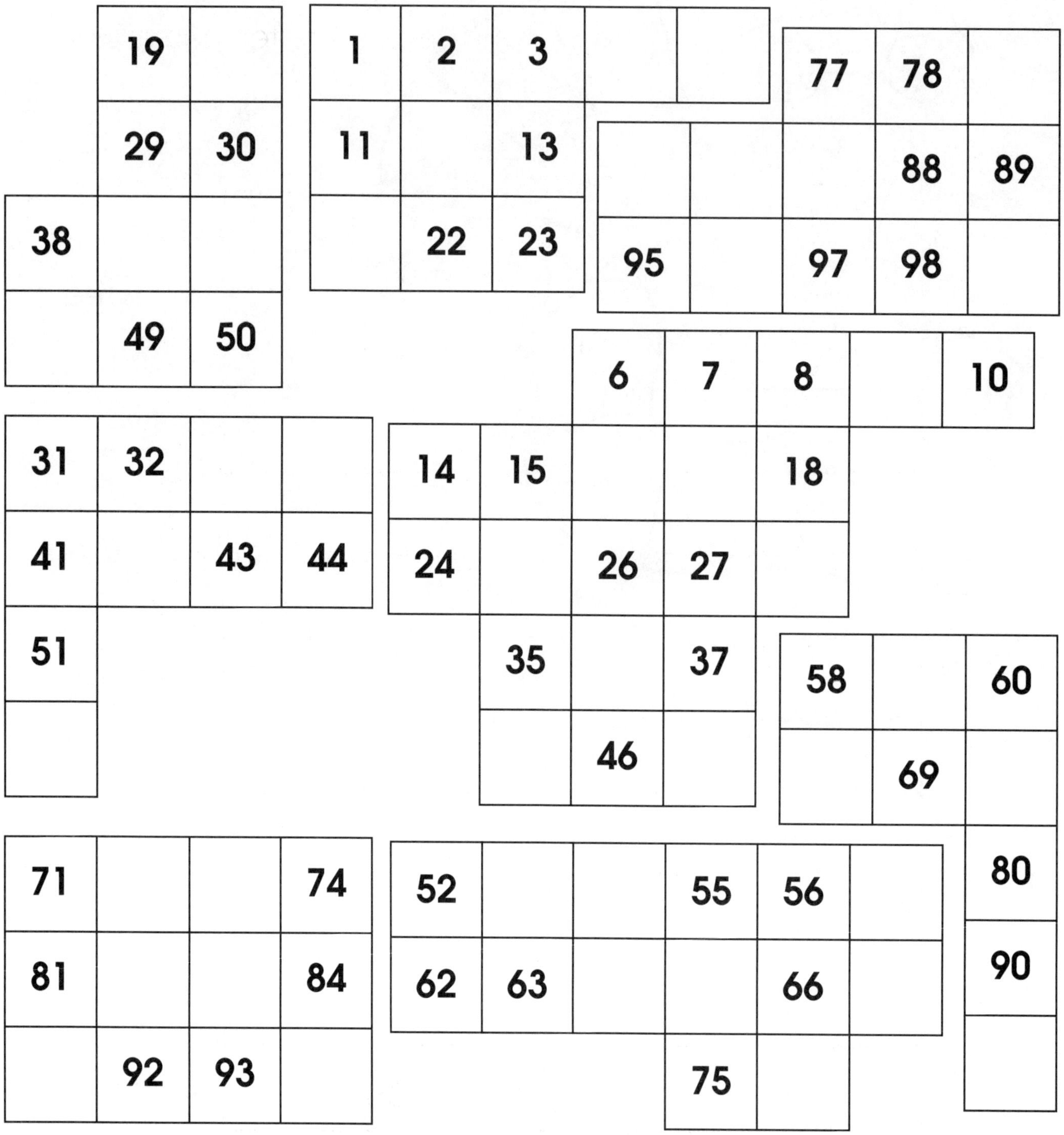

Name

Sequencing to 99

Unit 1

You can compare numbers by looking at the tens place of both numbers.

Example: 72 (greater) 56 (less)

The larger number is called **greater** and the smaller number is called **less**.
If the tens column is the same, go to the ones column.

Example: 36 (less) 39 (greater)

Help build the towers by making each number greater than the one below. Use the numbers in the clouds to help you.

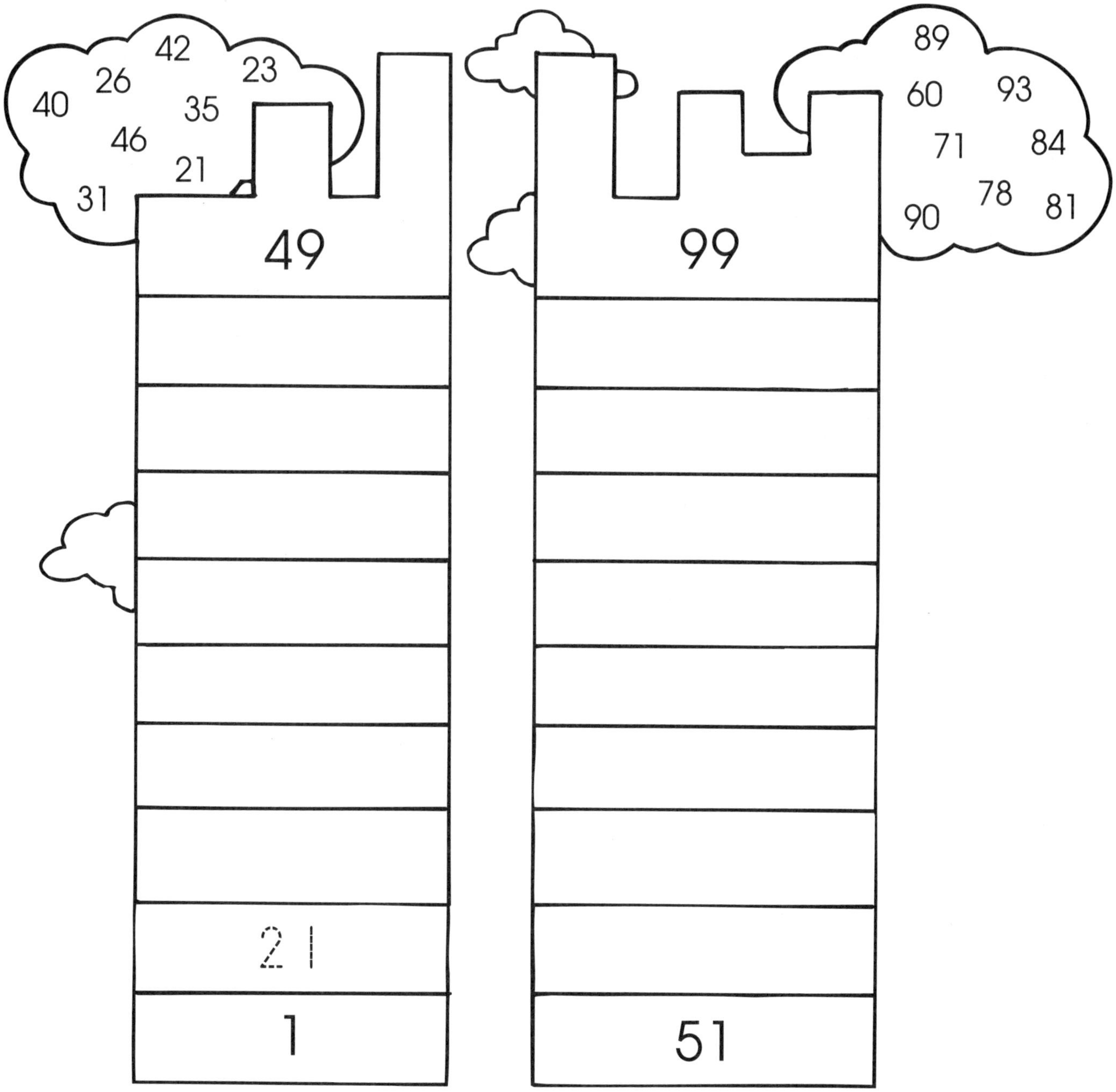

Name

Adding 10 **Unit 1**

Adding 10 to any number only changes the tens place.

Imagine adding one group of tens to each picture. How would the number change? Write the new number.

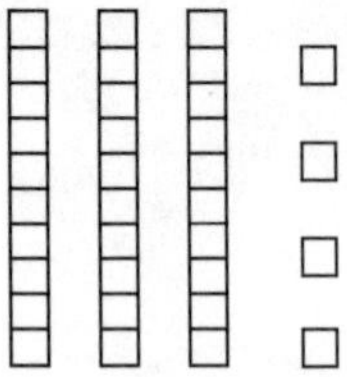

34 + 10 = 44

A.

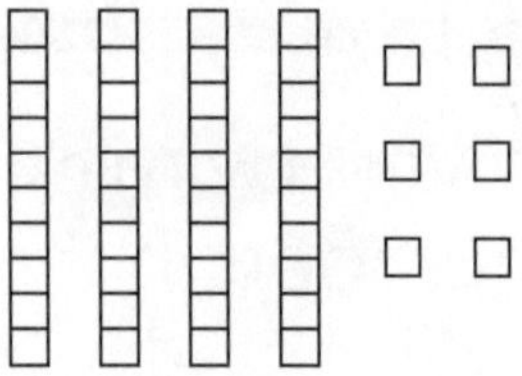

_______ + 10 = _______

B.

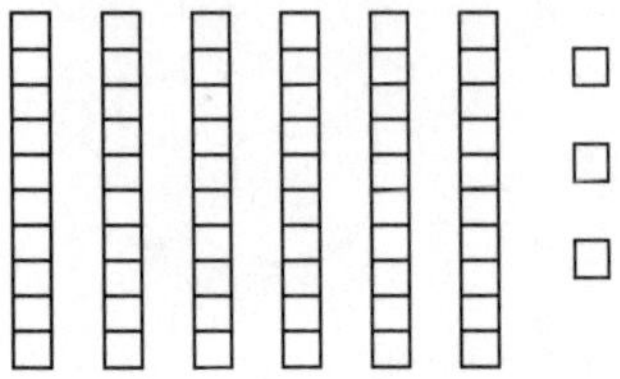

_______ + 10 = _______

C.

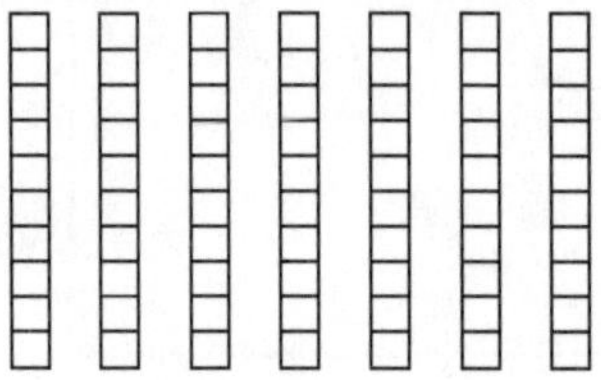

_______ + 10 = _______

D.

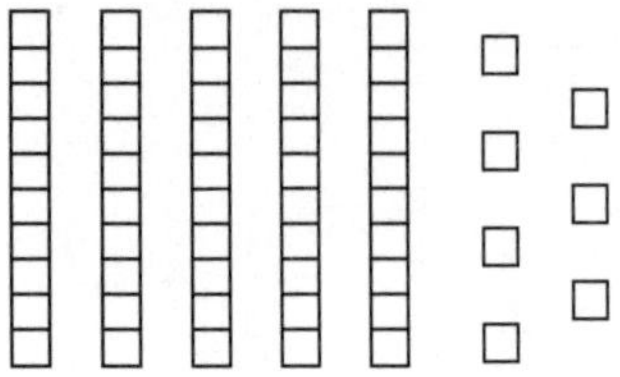

_______ + 10 = _______

E.

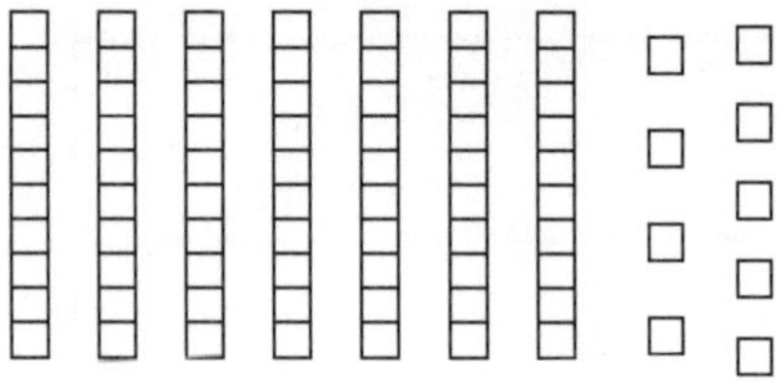

_______ + 10 = _______

Now try it without pictures.

F. 48 + 10 = ______ G. 35 + 10 = ______ H. 7 + 10 = ______

I. 72 + 10 = ______ J. 8 + 10 = ______ K. 84 + 10 = ______

L. 16 + 10 = ______ M. 59 + 10 = ______ N. 63 + 10 = ______

Name

Subtracting 10

Unit 1

Subtracting 10 from any number only changes the tens place.

Take 10 away from each picture. Write the new number.

33 – 10 = 23

A.

46 – 10 = _______

B.

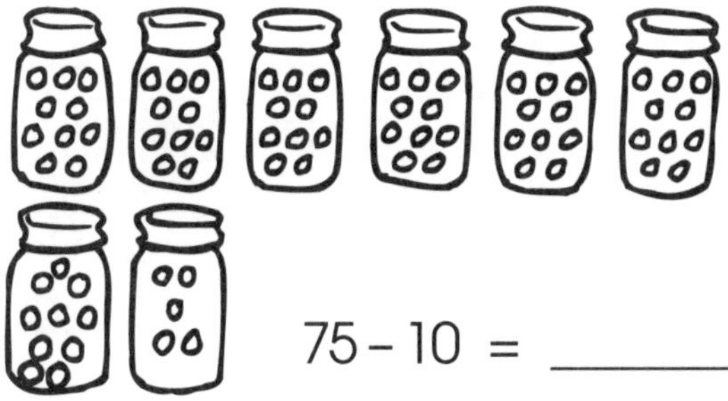

75 – 10 = _______

C.

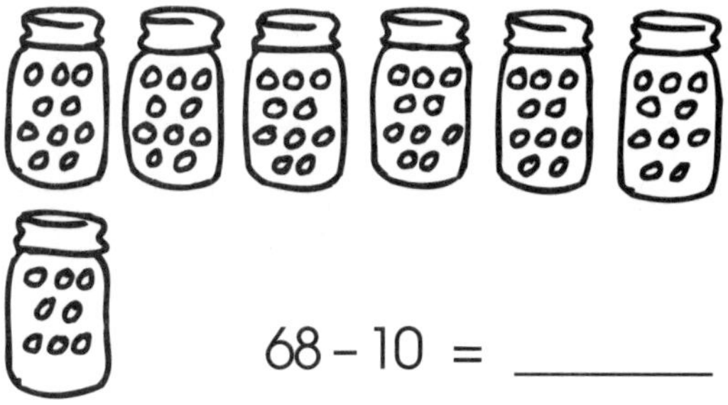

68 – 10 = _______

D.

90 – 10 = _______

E.

58 – 10 = _______

F. Complete the tables by subtracting 10 each time from the numbers on the left.

– 10	
59	49
46	
12	
74	

– 10	
65	
28	
83	
37	

Name

Counting by 5s and 10s

Unit 1

To count by 5, color every fifth number to make a pattern. To count by 10, color every tenth number to make a different pattern.

Count by 5s and color each number on the chart using a yellow crayon or marker. Now count by 10s and color each number using a red crayon or marker. What do you notice?

1	2	3	4	5	6	7	8	9	10
11	12	13	14	15	16	17	18	19	20
21	22	23	24	25	26	27	28	29	30
31	32	33	34	35	36	37	38	39	40
41	42	43	44	45	46	47	48	49	50
51	52	53	54	55	56	57	58	59	60
61	62	63	64	65	66	67	68	69	70
71	72	73	74	75	76	77	78	79	80
81	82	83	84	85	86	87	88	89	90
91	92	93	94	95	96	97	98	99	100

Fill in the missing numbers. You will be counting by 5s and 10s.

A.

5, ______, ______, 30, 35

B.

______, ______, 70, 80, 90, ______

C.

75, ☐, ☐, ☐, 95, ☐

D.

10, ☐, ☐, ☐, ☐, 60

E.

30, ☐, ☐, 45, 50, ☐, ☐, ☐

Name

Counting by 2s and 3s

Unit 1

To count by 2, color every second number to make a pattern. To count by 3, color every third number to make a different pattern.

A. Count by 2s. Color each number. What pattern do you see?

1	2	3	4	5	6	7	8	9	10
11	12	13	14	15	16	17	18	19	20
21	22	23	24	25	26	27	28	29	30
31	32	33	34	35	36	37	38	39	40

B. Now count by 3s. Color each number. How is this pattern different?

1	2	3	4	5	6	7	8	9	10
11	12	13	14	15	16	17	18	19	20
21	22	23	24	25	26	27	28	29	30
31	32	33	34	35	36	37	38	39	40

Fill in the missing numbers. You will be counting by 2s or 3s.

C.

9, 12, ________, 18, ________

D.

16, 18, ________, 22, ________

E.

☐, 10, 12, ☐, 16

F.

☐, 6, 9, ☐

G.

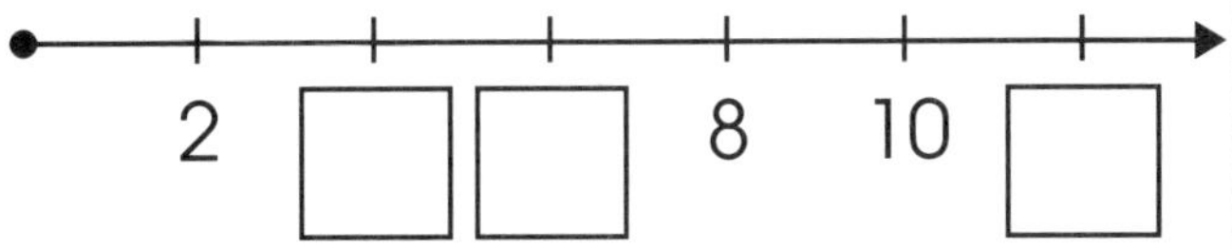

H.

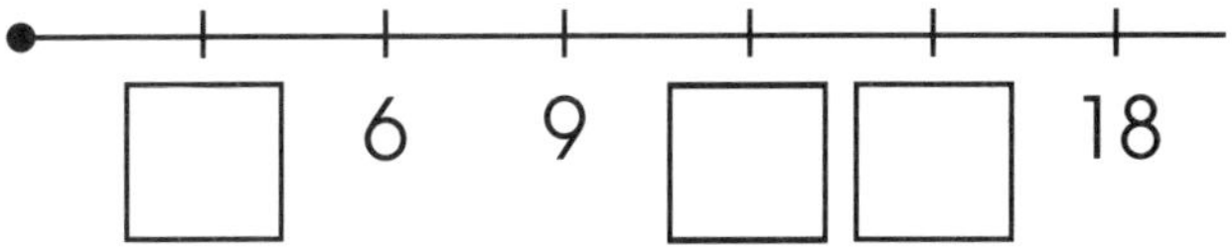

Name

Unit 1 Test

Page 1

Numeration Part I

Read or listen to the question. Fill in the circle beside the best answer.

Read all of the choices before you answer.

❑ Example:
Which number matches the number on the truck?

Ⓐ thirty-six Ⓑ 60 + 3

Ⓒ sixty Ⓓ 30 + 6

Answer: B because 60 + 3 is another way to write 63.

Now try these. You have 20 minutes. Continue until you see STOP.

1. How many blocks are there?

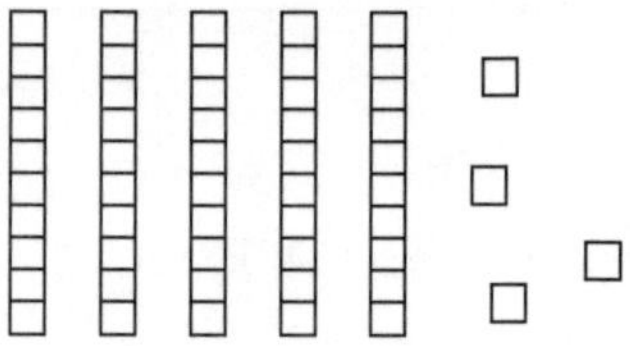

Ⓐ	Ⓑ	Ⓒ	Ⓓ
54	45	50	40

2. Which number shows another way to write 47?

Ⓐ	Ⓑ	Ⓒ	Ⓓ
40 + 4	70 + 4	70 + 7	40 + 7

3. Which number is seventy-eight?

Ⓐ	Ⓑ	Ⓒ	Ⓓ
68	87	78	88

GO ON

Name

Unit 1 Test

4. Which numbers are missing? 75, 76, ________, 78, 79, ________

Ⓐ 76 and 80

Ⓑ 77 and 80

Ⓒ 75 and 81

Ⓓ 77 and 81

5. Which man is the youngest?

Ⓐ 

Ⓑ 

Ⓒ 

Ⓓ 

6. Show the picture with 10 more than this picture.

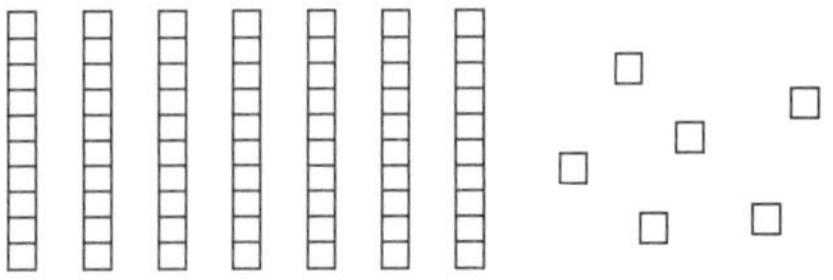

Ⓐ 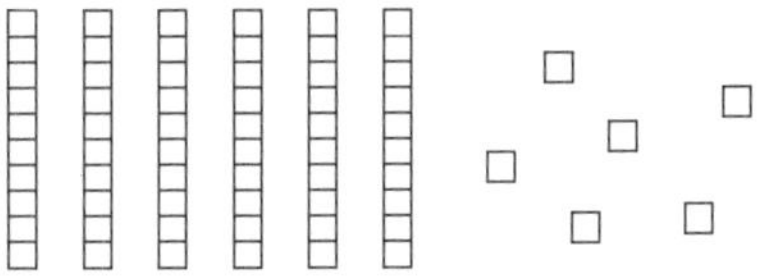

Ⓑ 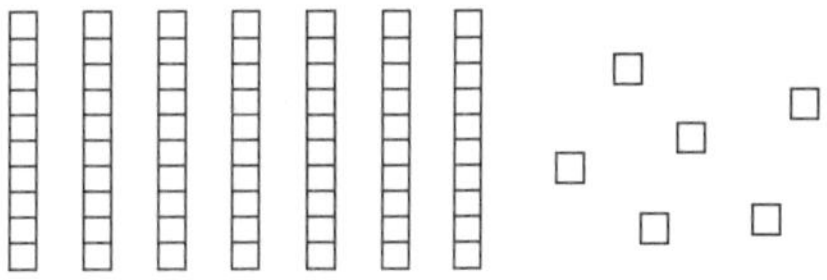

Ⓒ 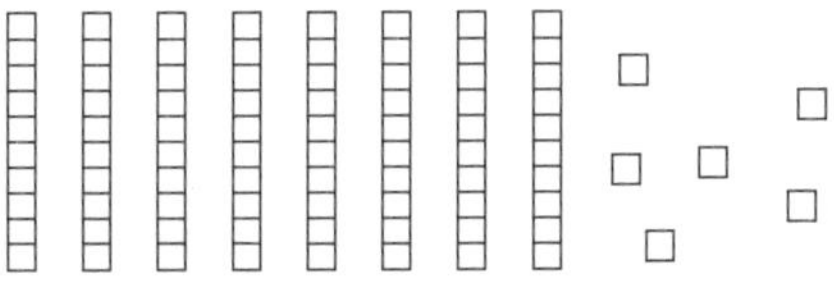

Ⓓ 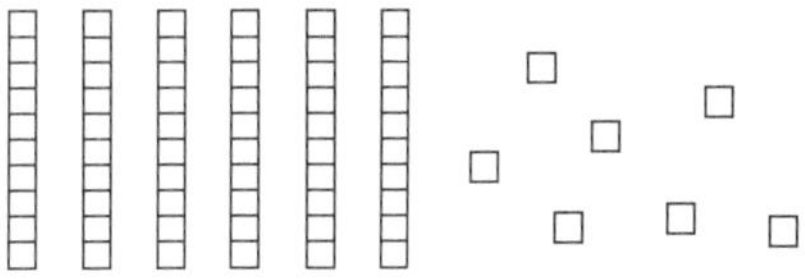

7. Which number is 10 less than 92?

Ⓐ 82

Ⓑ 93

Ⓒ 83

Ⓓ 90

8. Which number is missing?

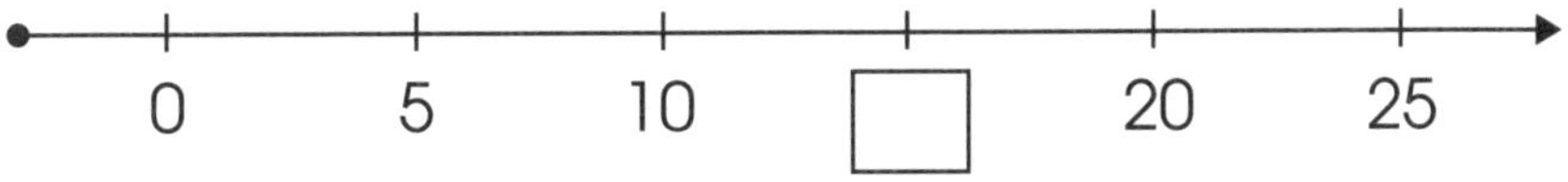

Ⓐ 20

Ⓑ 10

Ⓒ 15

Ⓓ 11

GO ON

Name

Unit 1 Test

9. Which numbers are missing? 9, 12, ______, ______, ______, 24

Ⓐ 13, 14, 15 Ⓑ 14, 16, 18 Ⓒ 15, 18, 21 Ⓓ 21, 22, 23

10. Which number has a 9 in the ones place?

Ⓐ 90 Ⓑ 94 Ⓒ 92 Ⓓ 29

11. Which number equals 20 + 6?

Ⓐ 22 Ⓑ 62 Ⓒ 20 Ⓓ 26

12. What page number is shown?

Ⓐ sixteen Ⓑ sixty-nine

Ⓒ ninety-six Ⓓ sixty

13. Which group shows counting by ones?

Ⓐ 48, 50, 51, 52 Ⓑ 49, 51, 50, 52

Ⓒ 48, 50, 52, 54 Ⓓ 48, 49, 50, 51

14. Which number is the greatest?

Ⓐ 40 Ⓑ 3 tens 2 ones Ⓒ forty-nine Ⓓ 30 + 8

GO ON

Name

Unit 1 Test

15. Which number shows 10 more than 35?

Ⓐ 40 + 5   Ⓑ 30 + 5   Ⓒ 10 + 5   Ⓓ 53

16. Which group shows 10 less than this picture?

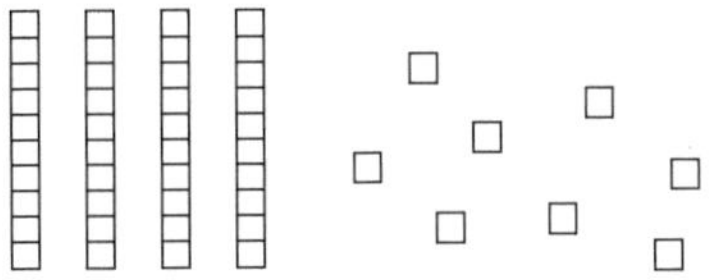

Ⓐ 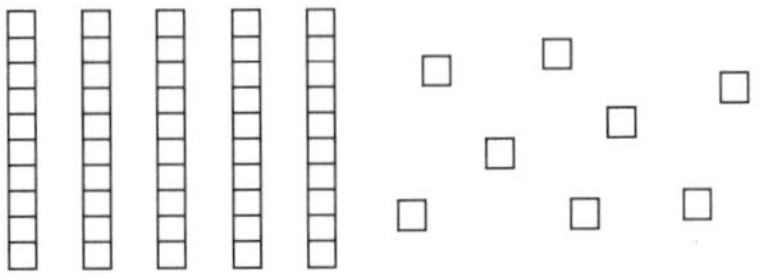

Ⓑ 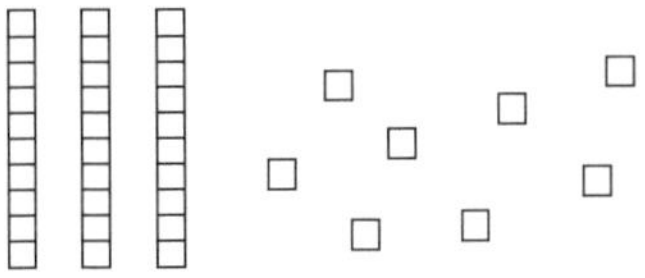

Ⓒ 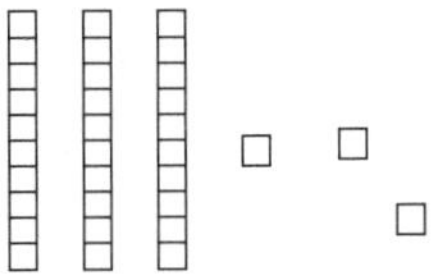

Ⓓ 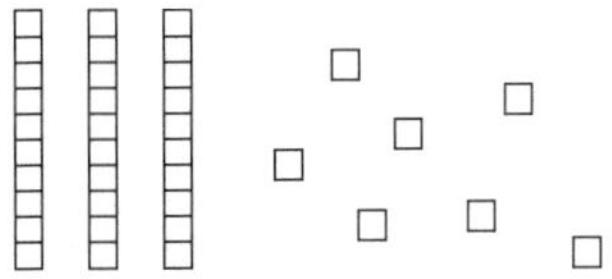

17. Which group shows counting by 10s?

Ⓐ 10, 15, 20   Ⓑ 20, 30, 60   Ⓒ 30, 40, 50   Ⓓ 10, 12, 14

18. Finish the number line.

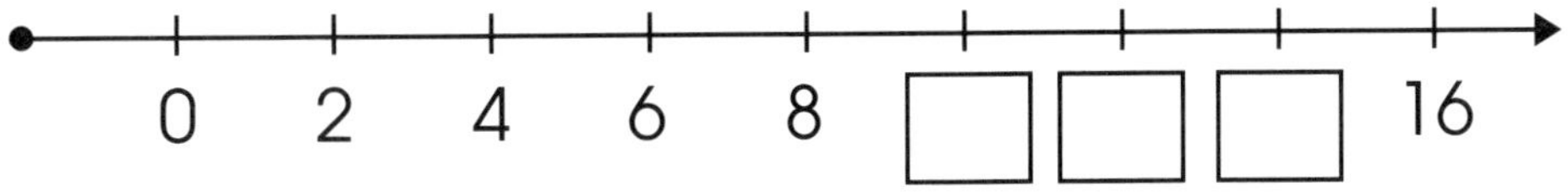

Ⓐ 10, 12, 14
Ⓑ 9, 10, 11
Ⓒ 10, 14, 18
Ⓓ 13, 14, 15

GO ON

Name

Unit 1 Test

19. Which ticket is number 71?

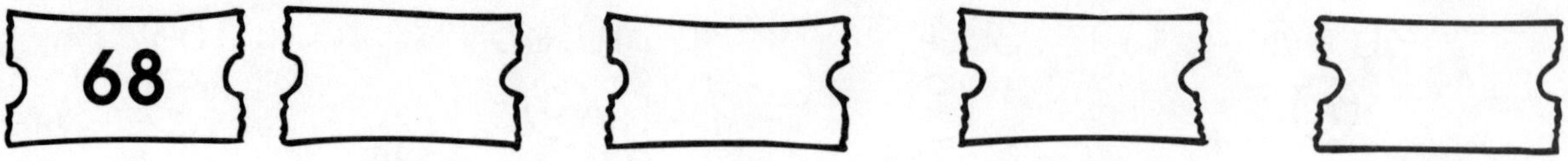

(A) (B) (C) (D)

20. Which number is between 80 and 85?

8 tens 2 ones	eighteen	80 + 9	58
(A)	(B)	(C)	(D)

Choose a number between 20 and 99. Write your number in the box. Now draw tens and ones blocks to show your number.

STOP

Name

Grouping of hundreds, tens, and ones

Unit 2

What is different about the numbers 99 and 100? 100 is called a 3-digit number because it has three parts: a hundreds place, a tens place, and a ones place.

Count the groups. Then write a 3-digit number two ways as shown.

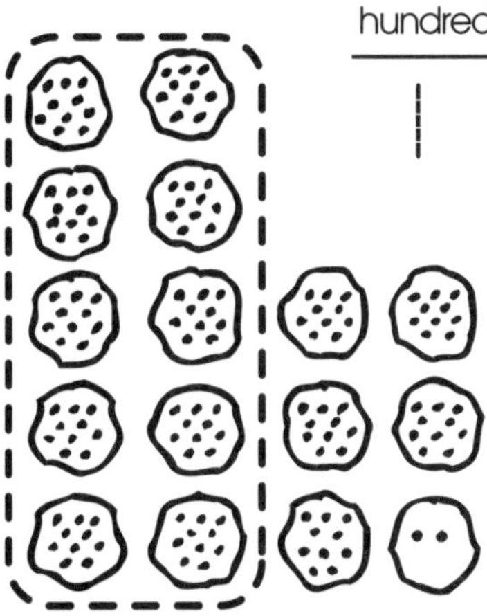

hundreds	tens	ones
1	5	2

152

A.

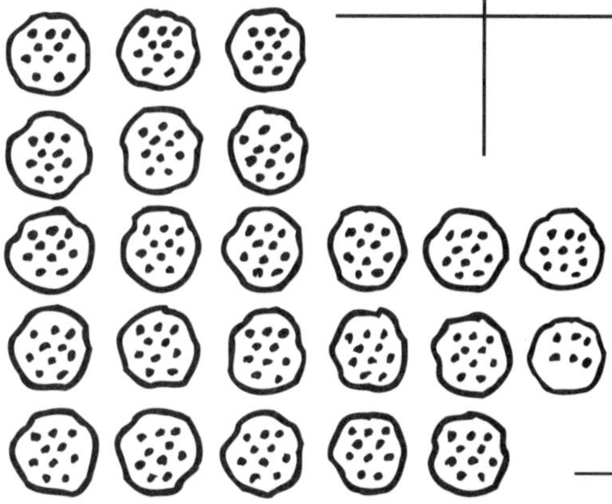

hundreds	tens	ones

____

B.

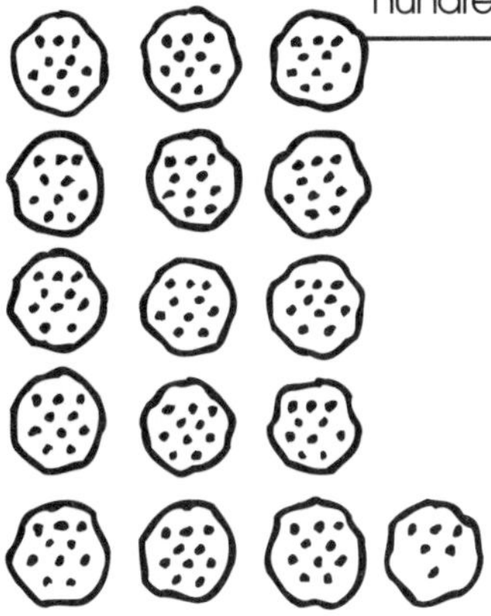

hundreds	tens	ones

____

C.

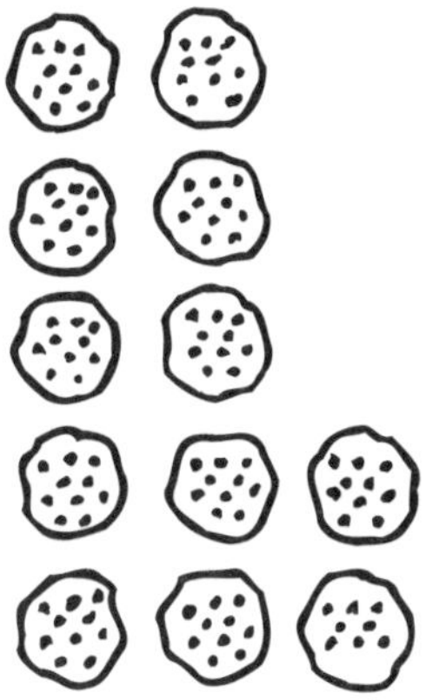

hundreds	tens	ones

____

D.

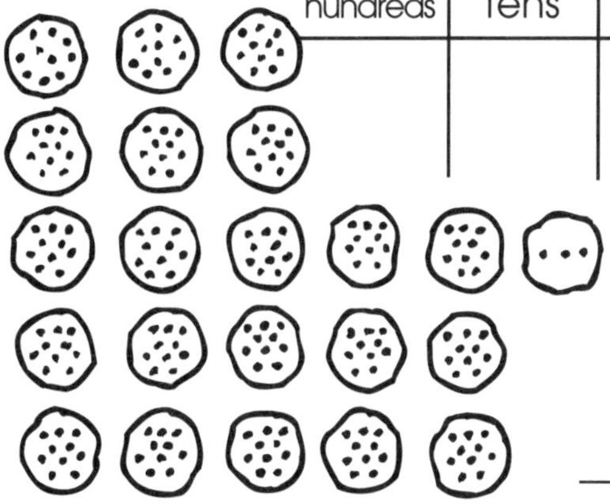

hundreds	tens	ones

____

E.

hundreds	tens	ones

____

Name

3-digit numbers in expanded notation

Unit 2

A 3-digit number can be written as an addition problem by separating the hundreds, tens, and ones. This is called **expanded notation**.

Write an addition problem for each picture as shown. Then write the number.

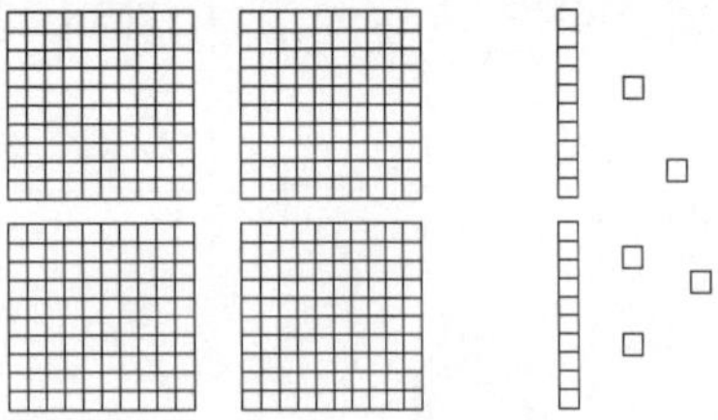

400 + 20 + 5

425

A.

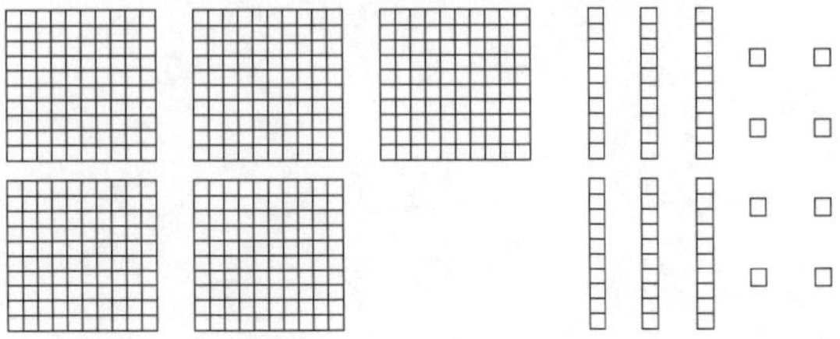

________ + ________ + ________

____

B.

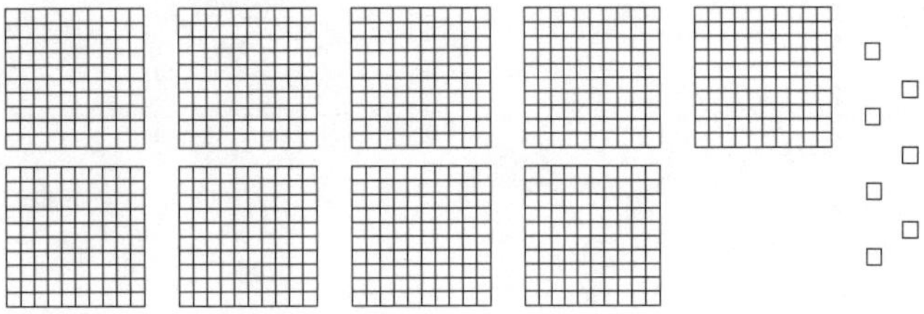

________ + ________ + ________

____

C.

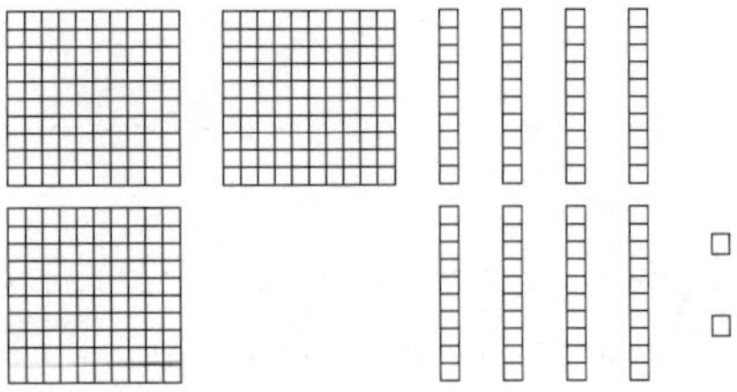

________ + ________ + ________

____

D.

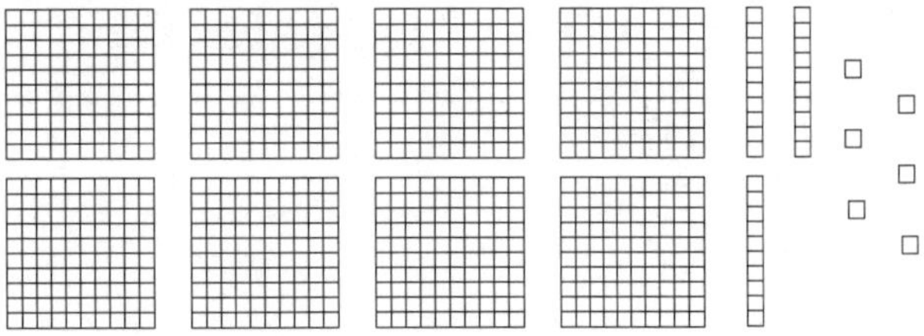

________ + ________ + ________

____

E.

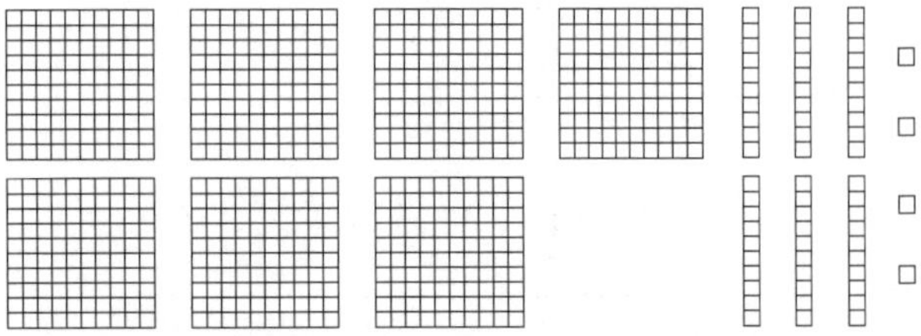

________ + ________ + ________

____

Name

3-digit number names

Unit 2

Numbers can be written in word form as well as numerals.

Find the written name for each number. Then use the code to answer the riddle.

Why didn't Benjamin Franklin speak when he experimented with electricity?

____ ____   ____ ____ ____   ____ ____

110 798   476 856 998   101 206

____ ____ ____ ____ ____ !

998 110 202 467 685

eight hundred fifty-six **A**	seven hundred ninety-eight **E**
one hundred one **I**	four hundred sixty-seven **C**
one hundred ten **H**	nine hundred ninety-eight **S**
four hundred seventy-six **W**	two hundred six **n**
two hundred two **O**	six hundred eighty-five **K**

Name

Sequencing to 999

Unit 2

To find the correct order of 3-digit numbers, always look at the hundreds place first. The number with the most hundreds is the greatest number. If the numbers in the hundreds place are the same, go to the tens place. If they are the same, go to the ones. The higher number may be called greater, greatest, or most. The lower number may be called least, less, or lowest.

Write the matching number in each box. Then sequence the numbers from least to greatest on the lines at the bottom.

A.

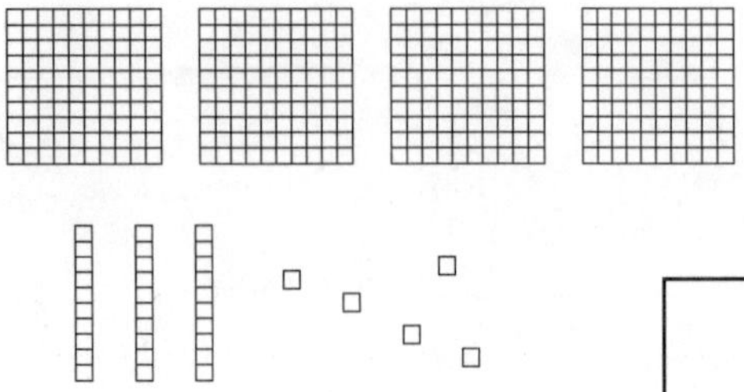

B.
7 hundreds
6 tens
8 ones

C.
nine hundred ten

D.
300 + 70 + 8

E.

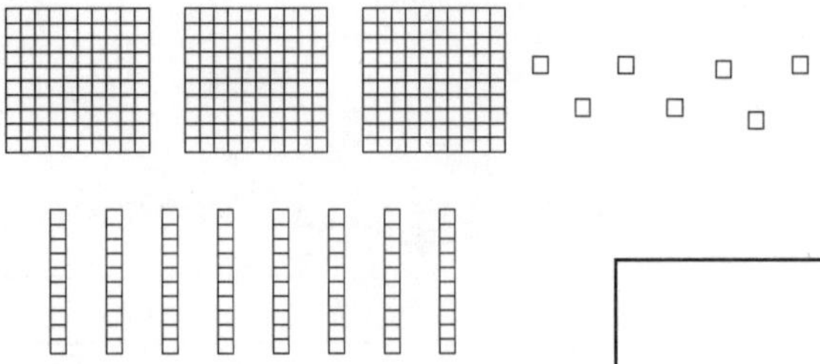

F.
one hundred ninety-nine

G.

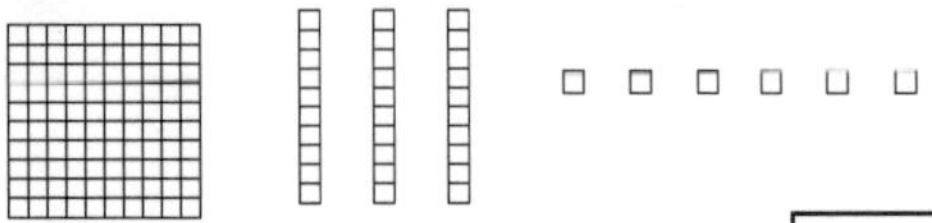

H.
6 hundreds
8 tens
3 ones

I.
600 + 10 + 4

J.
eight hundred fifteen

K. Least   Greatest

136, ______, ______, ______, ______, ______, ______, ______, ______, ______

Name

Adding and subtracting 100

Unit 2

Adding and subtracting groups of hundreds only changes the hundreds place.

Scientists are always looking at our changing star patterns. Imagine hundreds of new stars being discovered while hundreds of others burn out.

Complete the star chart by adding and subtracting 100.

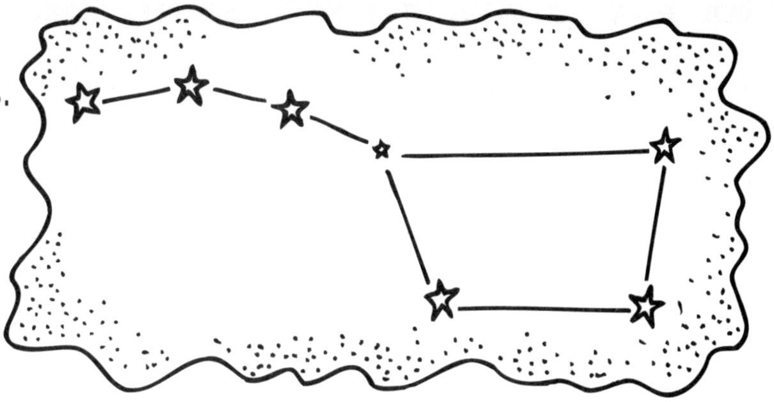

	Number of ★ Before	+ Discovered ★	= Number of ★ Now
A.	881	+ 100	
B.	763	+ 200	
C.	405	+ 300	
D.	312	+ 400	

	Number of ★ Before	– Burned Out ★	= Number of ★ Now
E.	962	– 200	
F.	814	– 300	
G.	730	– 400	
H.	689	– 500	
I.	978	– 600	

Name

Ordinal numbers

Unit 2

When objects are in a particular order, they can be assigned **ordinal numbers**: first, second, third, etc. Always check closely to find the front of the line!

Complete each sentence using the words in the sun.

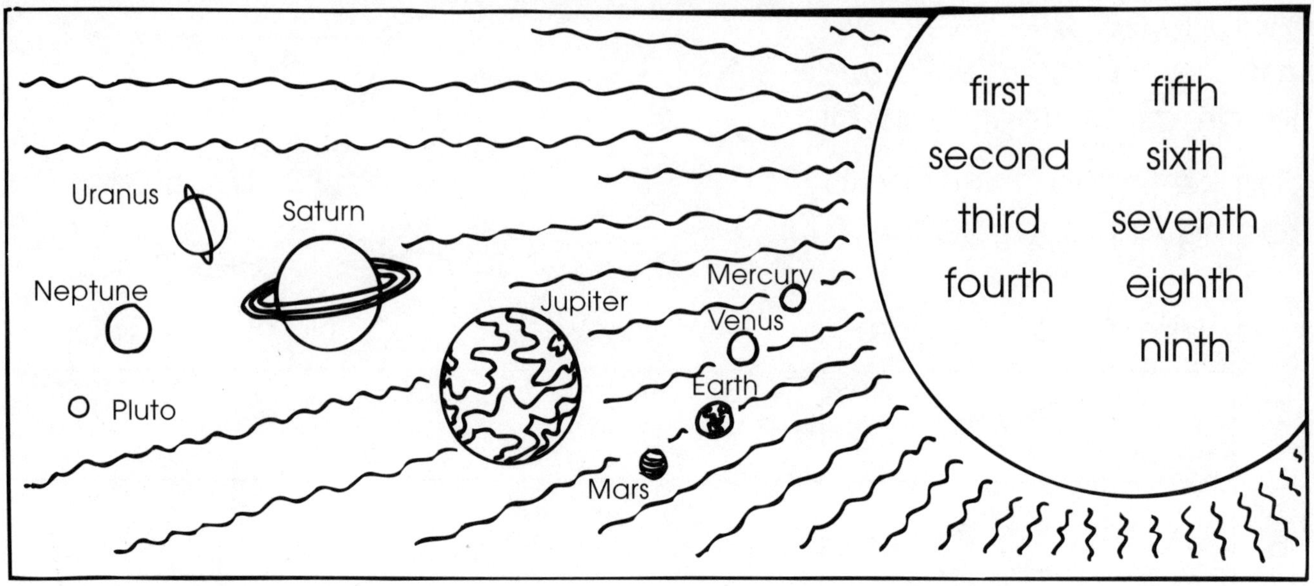

A. Mars is the ________________ planet from the sun.

B. Jupiter is the ________________ planet from the sun.

C. Pluto is the ________________ planet from the sun.

D. Venus is the ________________ planet from the sun.

E. Mercury is the ________________ planet from the sun.

F. Saturn is the ________________ planet from the sun.

G. Earth is the ________________ planet from the sun.

H. Uranus is the ________________ planet from the sun.

I. Neptune is the ________________ planet from the sun.

Name

Even/odd numbers

Unit 2

Even numbers end in 0, 2, 4, 6, or 8. **Odd numbers** end in 1, 3, 5, 7, or 9.

Find Steven's path home by coloring the even numbers.

Name

Rounding to the nearest ten

Unit 2

Rounding means estimating. Rounding to the nearest ten means estimating using the number in the ones place. The rule for rounding to the nearest ten is:

When you see 1, 2, 3, or 4 in the ones place, you will round ⇩.
When you see 5, 6, 7, 8, or 9 in the ones place, you will round ⇧.

Examples: 1<u>3</u> rounds to 10   1<u>5</u> rounds to 20

This wacky store will only allow you to pay in dimes (amounts of tens). Round each price tag to the nearest ten to decide the price.

0 1 2 3 4 5 6 7 8 9

Round ⇩. ←   → Round ⇧.

A. 64¢ ☐

B. 73¢ ☐

C. 78¢ ☐

D. 89¢ ☐

E. 56¢ ☐

F. 24¢ ☐

G. 37¢ ☐

H. 42¢ ☐

I. 15¢ ☐

J. 45¢ ☐

K. 91¢ ☐

L. 82¢ ☐

M. 27¢ ☐

N. 11¢ ☐

O. 68¢ ☐

P. 75¢ ☐

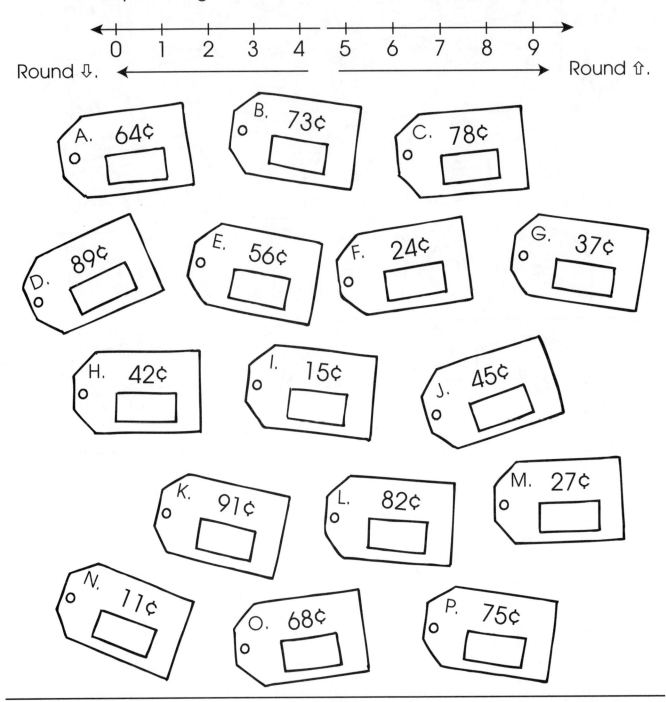

Name

Rounding to the nearest hundred

Unit 2

Rounding means estimating. Rounding to the nearest hundred means estimating using the number in the tens or ones place. The rule for rounding to the nearest hundred is:

When you see 0, 1, 2, 3, or 4 in the tens place, you will round ⇩.
When you see 5, 6, 7, 8, or 9 in the tens place, you will round ⇧.

Examples: 1<u>3</u>4 rounds to 100   1<u>8</u>3 rounds to 200

The elevator has gone mad! Draw an arrow to show which way to round the number to the nearest hundred. Then write the rounded number.

0 1 2 3 4 | 5 6 7 8 9

Round ⇩. ⟵   ⟶ Round ⇧.

258	↑	300
722		
648		
391		
928		
453		
137		
558		

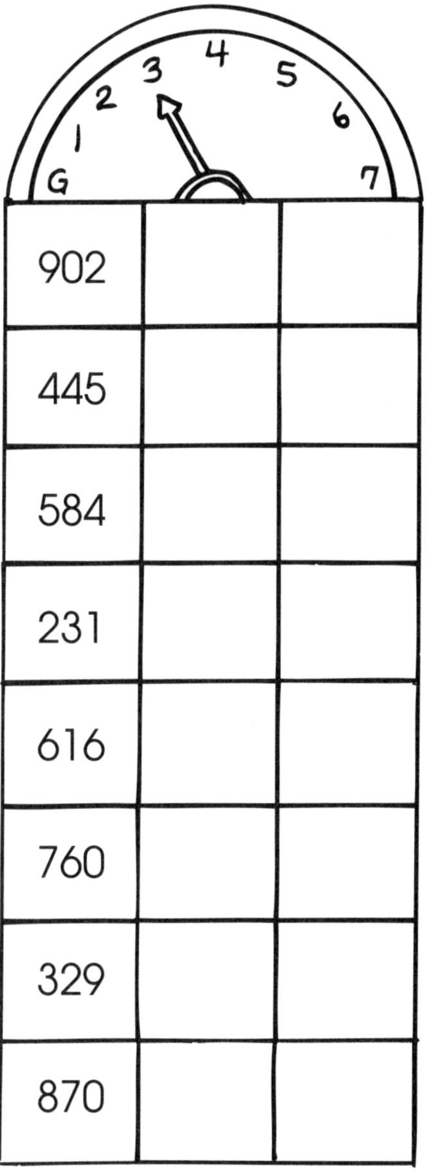

902		
445		
584		
231		
616		
760		
329		
870		

Name

Naming numbers using clues **Unit 2**

Numbers are named and described in a variety of ways. Use this puzzle to sharpen your skills.

Use the clues to complete the puzzle. The answer choices are in the Number Bank.

Across

1. I am an odd number. My digits add up to six.
3. I am an odd number. I am between 100 and 200.
4. I am even. I could be rounded to 900.
6. I am even. I have a 3 in the hundreds place.
8. I am even. I have no ones.
9. I am odd. My digits add up to 14.

Down

2. I am even. The hundreds and tens digits are the same.
5. I am odd. My digits add up to 7.
7. I am even. I have a 9 in the tens place.
9. I am odd. I have a 9 in the tens place.

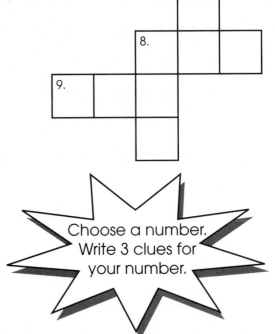

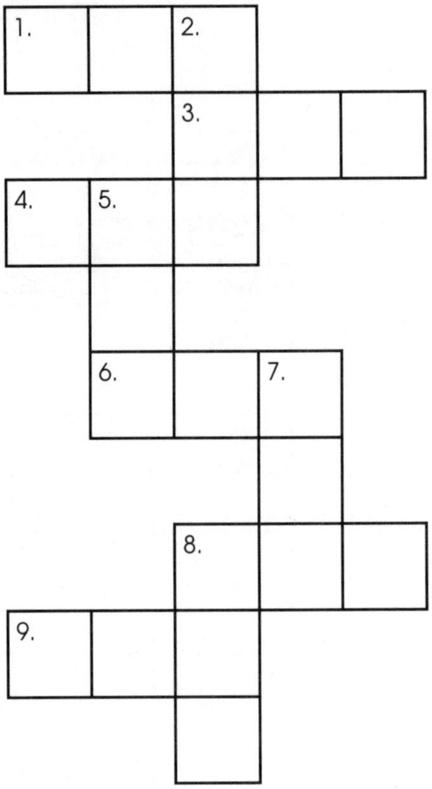

175 118 372

948 296 419

960 403 997

321

Choose a number. Write 3 clues for your number.

Name

Unit 2 Test

Page 1

Numeration Part II

Read or listen to the question. Fill in the circle beside the best answer.

Cross out
answers you
know are
wrong.

❑ Example:
Which number is closest to 37?

Ⓐ 40 Ⓑ 30

Ⓒ 70 Ⓓ 50

Answer: A because the ones place has a 7, which tells you to round up to the nearest ten.

Now try these. You have 20 minutes. Continue until you see STOP.

1. How many marbles are there?

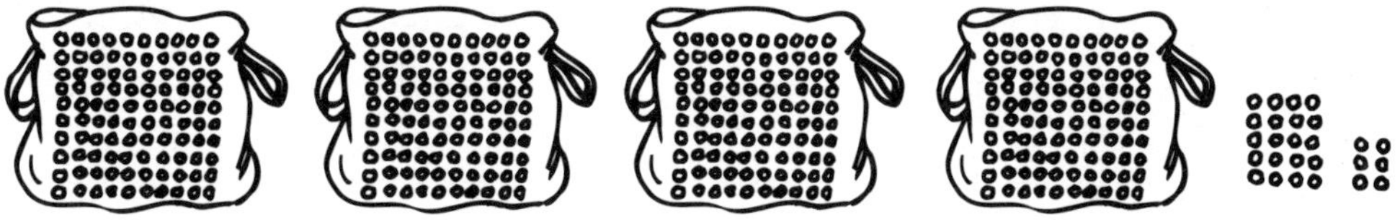

246	426	642	406
Ⓐ	Ⓑ	Ⓒ	Ⓓ

2. Which number shows the expanded notation for 837?

Ⓐ 300 + 80 + 7 Ⓑ 700 + 30 + 8

Ⓒ 300 + 70 + 8 Ⓓ 800 + 30 + 7

3. Which of these numbers would not be rounded to 30?

31	34	29	38
Ⓐ	Ⓑ	Ⓒ	Ⓓ

GO ON

Name

Unit 2 Test

4. Which number shows 200 more than 763?

Ⓐ 563 Ⓑ 783 Ⓒ 963 Ⓓ 936

5. Which number is the greatest?

Ⓐ 300 + 70 + 5

Ⓑ three hundred fifteen

Ⓒ

H	T	O
3	1	3

Ⓓ 3 hundreds, 2 tens, 6 ones

6. Mark the mouse that is fifth from the cheese.

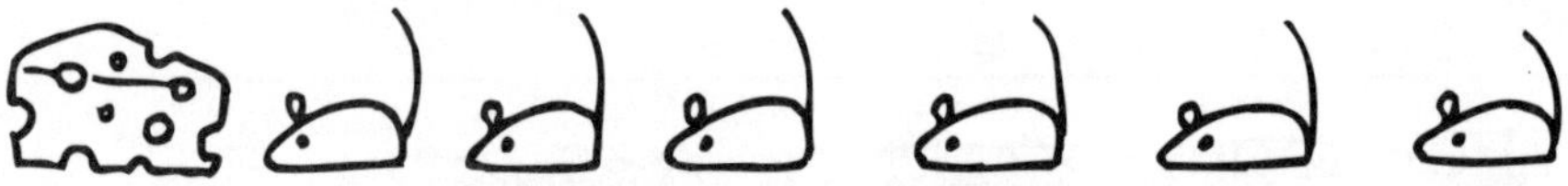

Ⓐ Ⓑ Ⓒ Ⓓ

7. Which number is not an even number?

Ⓐ 6 Ⓑ 9 Ⓒ 10 Ⓓ 14

8. Round 38 to the nearest ten.

Ⓐ 40 Ⓑ 80 Ⓒ 30 Ⓓ 380

9. Solve the riddle.

I can be rounded to 40. I am an even number. My digits add up to 6.

Ⓐ 48 Ⓑ 42

Ⓒ 41 Ⓓ 43

GO ON

Name

Unit 2 Test

10. Round 263 to the nearest hundred.

260	200	360	300
(A)	(B)	(C)	(D)

11. Which number has a 9 in the hundreds place?

429	492	942	249
(A)	(B)	(C)	(D)

12. Which number equals 500 + 60 + 3?

563	536	503	653
(A)	(B)	(C)	(D)

13. How many miles is it to New York?

(A) six hundred ninety

(B) six hundred nine

(C) six hundred nineteen

(D) nine hundred six

14. Which number is the least?

(A) 700 + 10 + 2

(B) seven hundred forty-five

(C) 7 hundreds, 3 tens, 7 ones

(D)

H	T	O
7	4	8

GO ON

Name

Unit 2 Test

Page 4

15. Mark the picture with 300 less than:

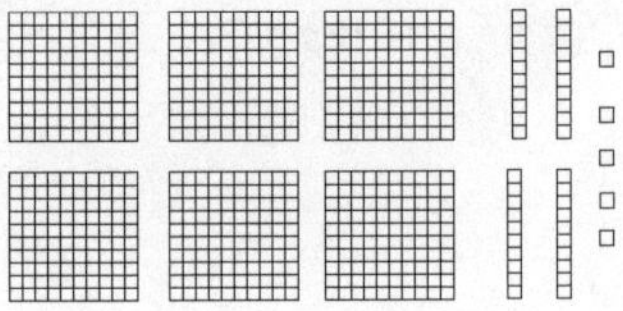

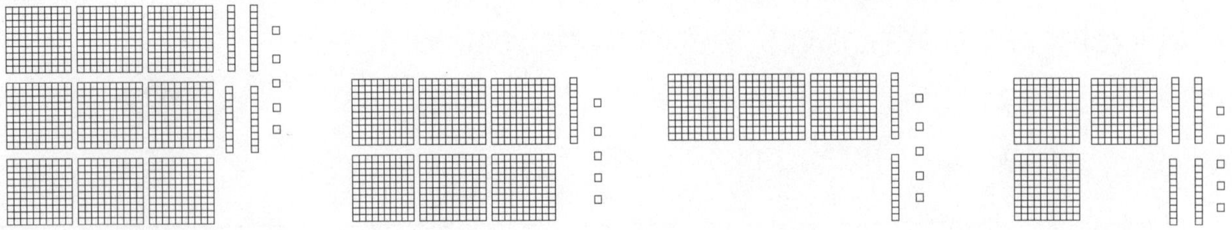

Ⓐ Ⓑ Ⓒ Ⓓ

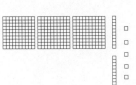

16. What odd number is in the triangle and the rectangle?

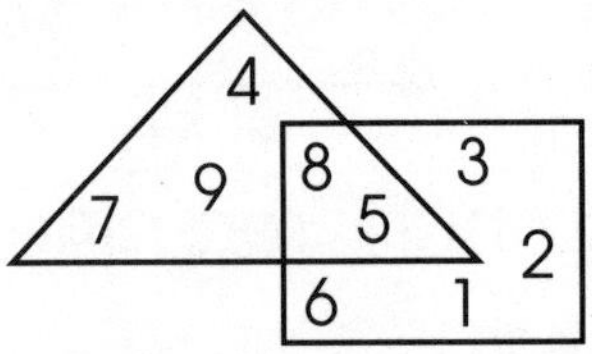

3	8	5	9
Ⓐ	Ⓑ	Ⓒ	Ⓓ

17. In what place is the train?

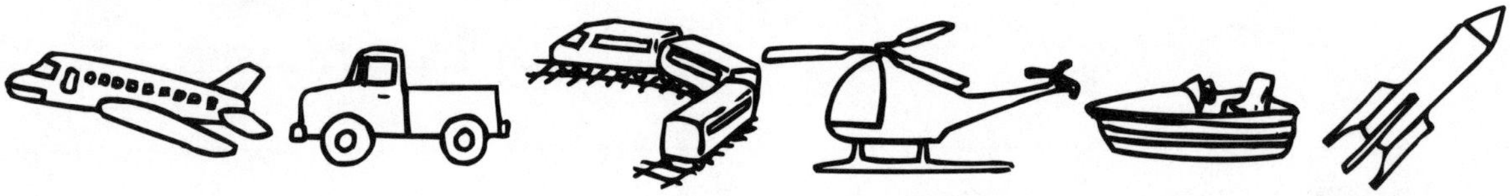

third	fourth	fifth	sixth
Ⓐ	Ⓑ	Ⓒ	Ⓓ

18. Which number is seven hundred eighty-two?

872	728	782	278
Ⓐ	Ⓑ	Ⓒ	Ⓓ

GO ON

Name

Unit 2 Test

Page 5

19. Which number can be rounded to 500?

586	412	592	486
(A)	(B)	(C)	(D)

20. Solve the riddle.

I can be rounded to 600.
I am an odd number.
My digits add up to 9.

(A) 606 (B) 603

(C) 360 (D) 663

Show three ways to write the number that is ten more than 362.

STOP

Name

Plane figures

Unit 3

Plane figures are shapes that are flat.

Color the plane figures as described.

square in a circle = yellow
triangle in a triangle = red
rectangle in an oval = brown
circle in a square = blue
triangle in a rectangle = green
circle in a circle = orange

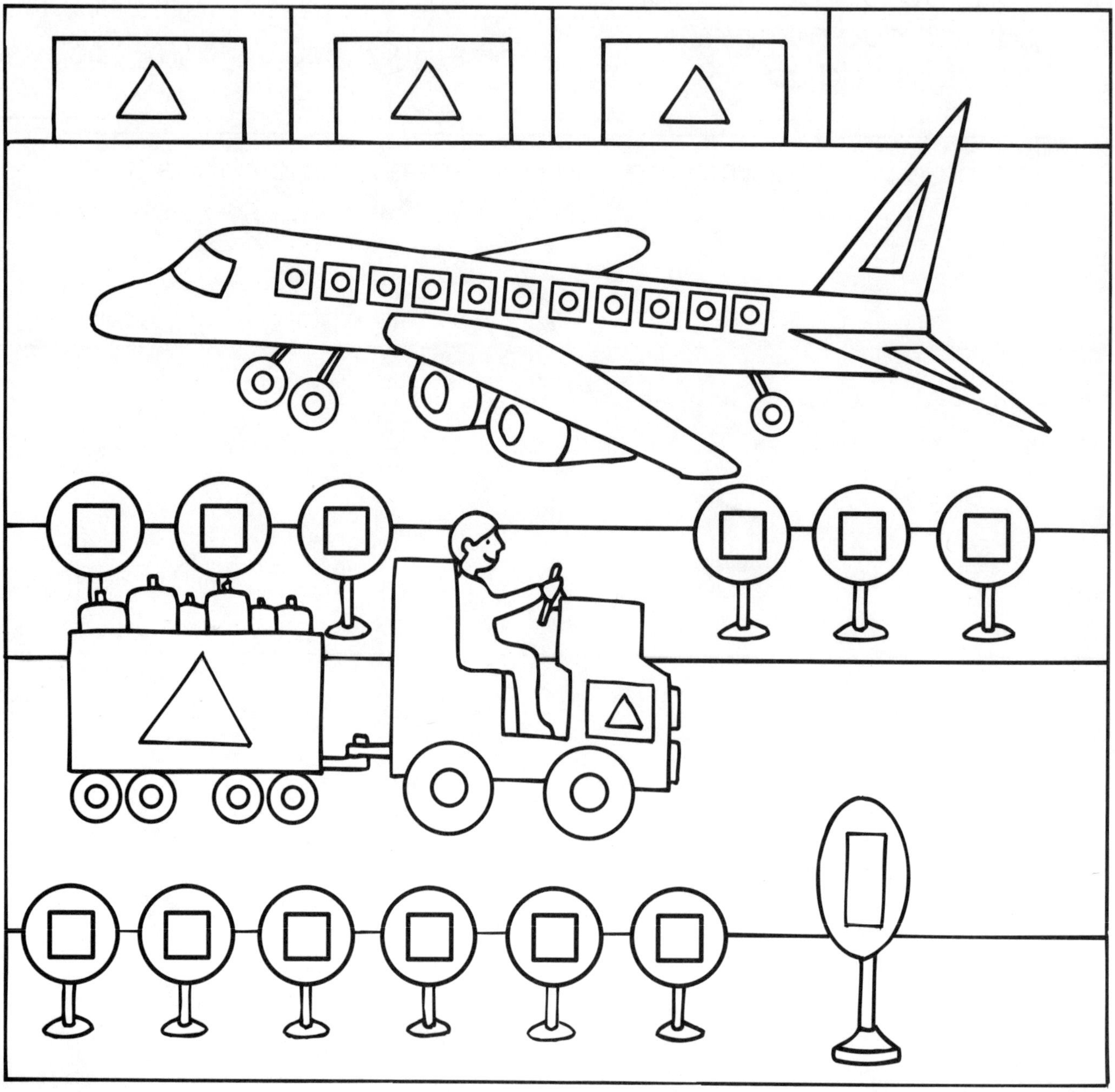

Name

Solid figures

Unit 3

Shapes that are 3-dimensional are called **solid**. A round solid shape is not called a circle, it is called a sphere. Look at the solid figures and their names in the chart.

Count each solid figure in the picture below. Then color the boxes in the graph to show how many of each figure you found.

6					
5					
4					
3					
2					
1					
	sphere	cube	cone	rectangular prism	cylinder

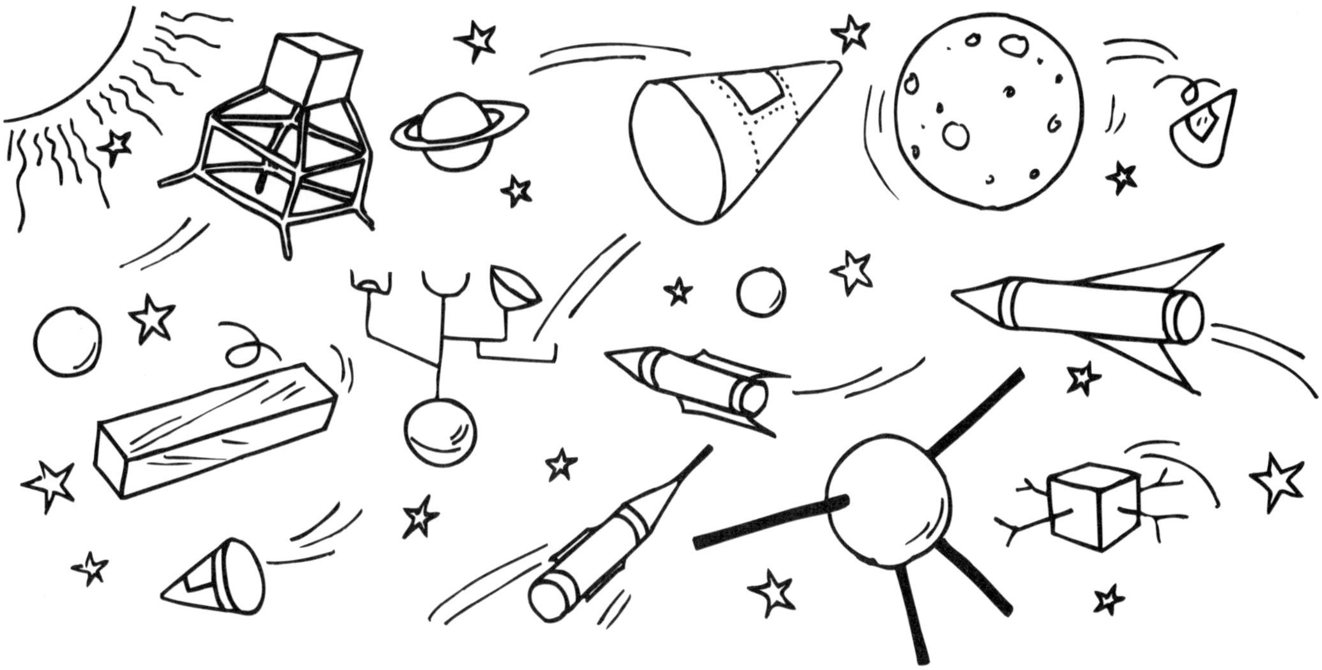

Find an object in the classroom that resembles a sphere, a cube, a cone, a rectangular prism, and a cylinder.

Name

Endpoints, angles, line segments

Unit 3

Many plane and spatial figures have:

line segments  angles 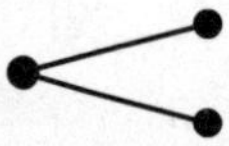 endpoints 

Complete the chart by counting the line segments, angles, and endpoints.

Shape	Draw the figure.	# Endpoints	# Line segments	# Angles
A. square				
B. rectangle				
C. diamond				
D. octagon				
E. triangle				

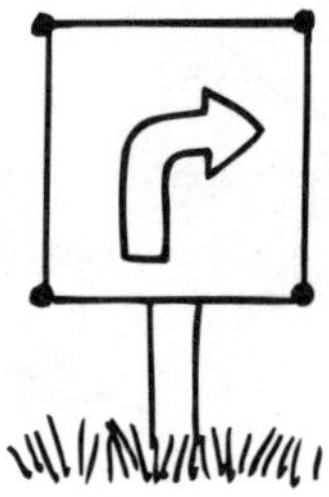

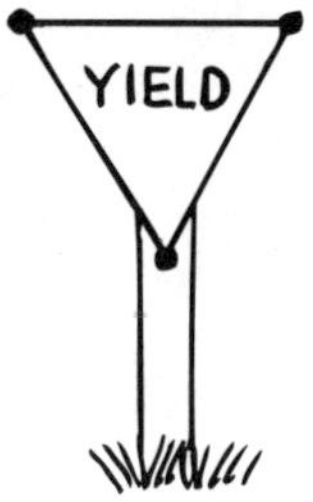

Name

Congruent reflections

Unit 3

Congruent means exactly the same size and shape. Two congruent shapes may be lying in different directions, but their sizes and shapes must match.

Example:

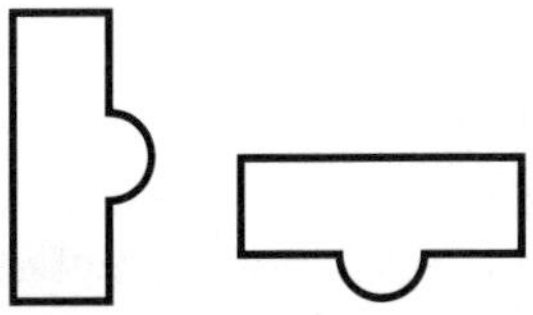

Label the pieces **1**, **2**, **3**, and **4** to match their spots in the puzzle.

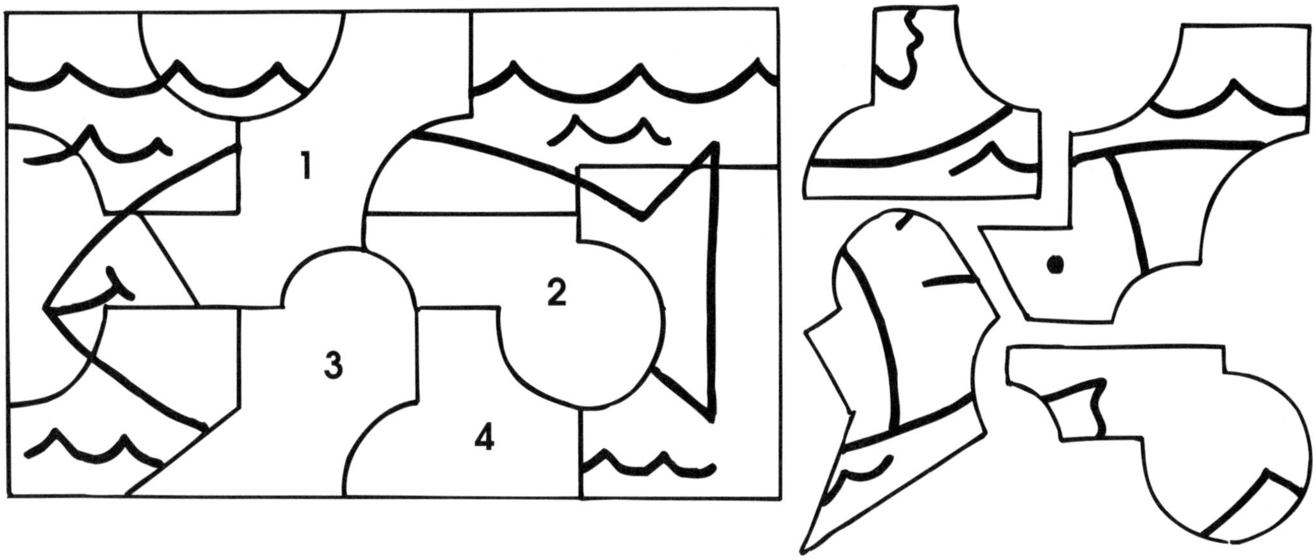

A **reflection** is a mirrored image. The size and shape of the figure stays the same, but the direction is reversed.
Example:

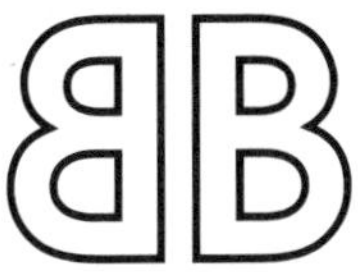

Draw the reflection of each picture in the mirror.

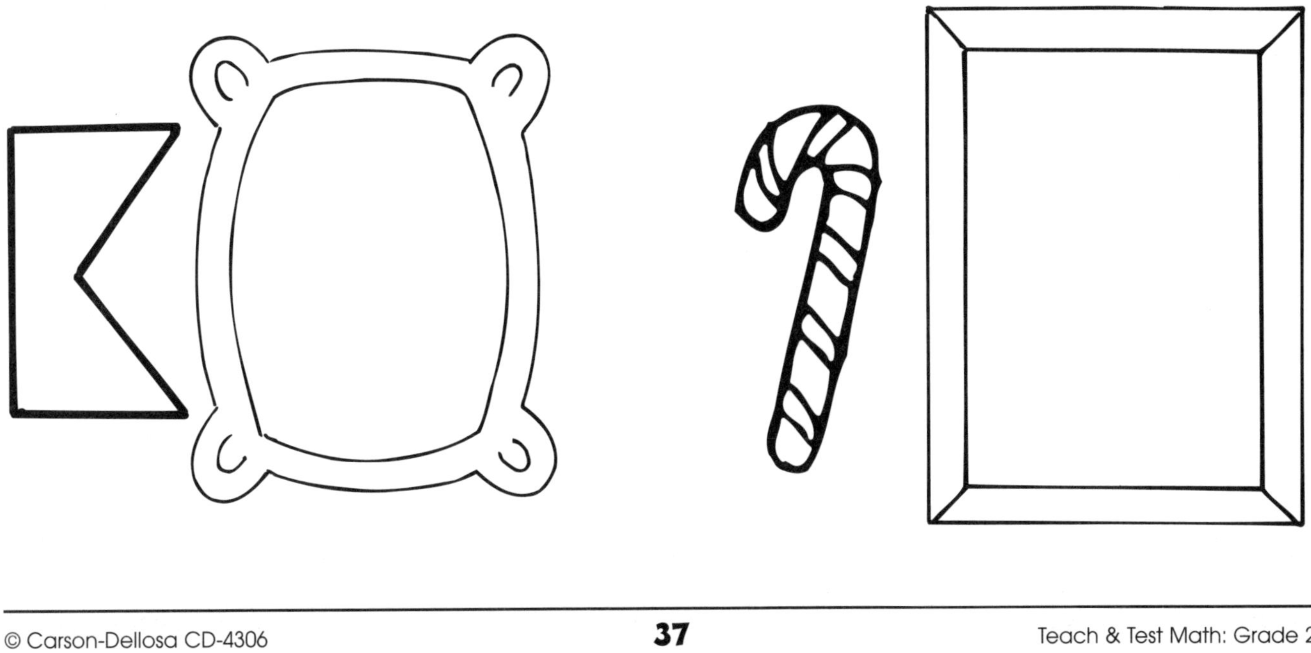

Name

Congruent rotations

Unit 3

Place the tip of your pencil on the dot in the center of the picture. Without picking up your pencil, turn your paper and look at the picture. How has it changed? This is called **rotating**.

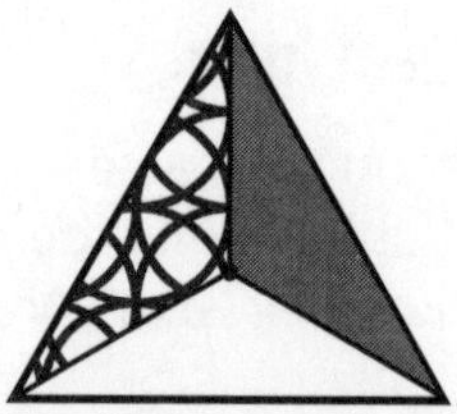

Imagine rotating each shape. Which picture does not show part of the rotation? Put an **X** on the picture.

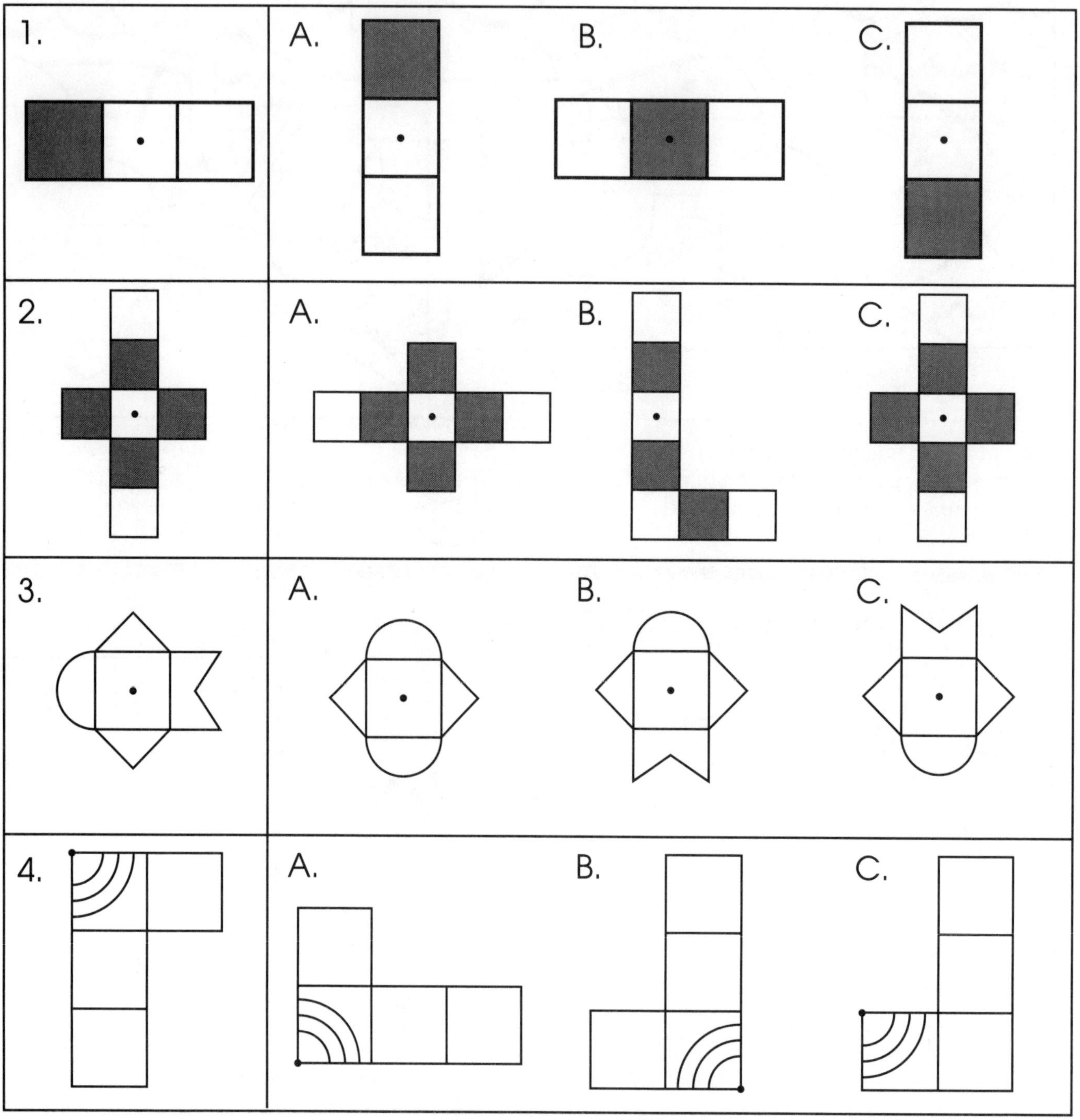

Name

Lines of symmetry

Unit 3

Imagine folding or drawing a line on each figure below so that both sides are identical. The fold or line is called the **line of symmetry**. Some figures have more than one line of symmetry.

Examples:

Lines of symmetry:

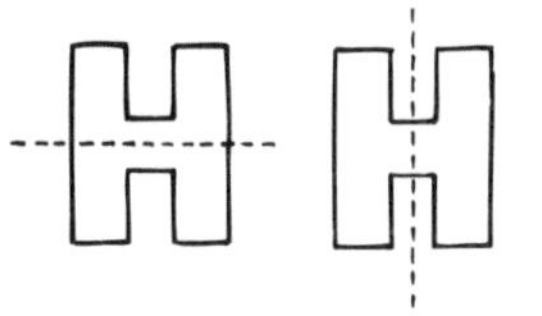

Not lines of symmetry:

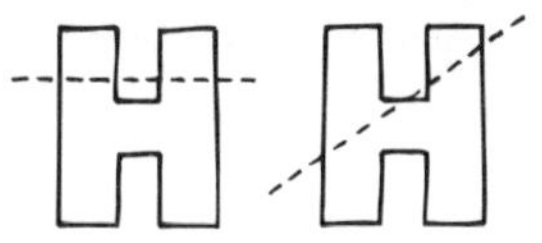

Draw all the lines of symmetry for these figures.

Name

Calculating perimeter

Unit 3

Perimeter is the distance around the outside of a figure.

Example:

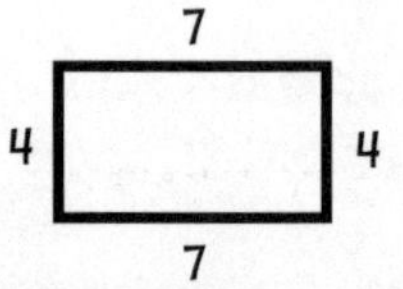

7 + 7 + 4 + 4 = 22 units

Add the lengths of the sides to find the perimeters.

A.

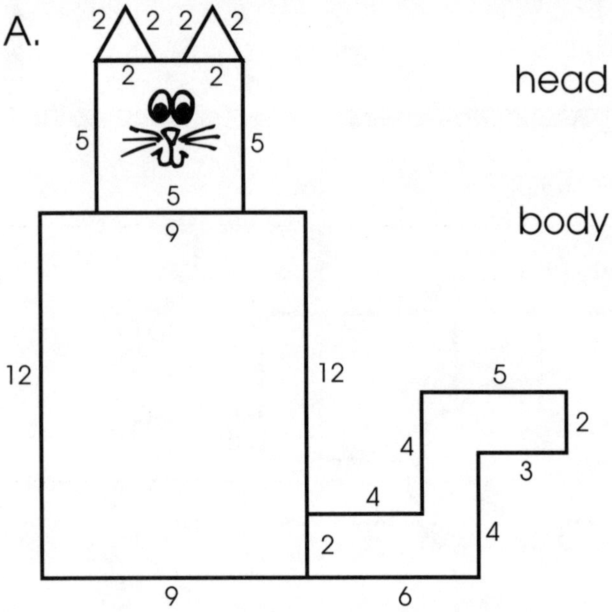

head = ____ + ____ + ____ + ____ = ☐ units

body = ____ + ____ + ____ + ____ = ☐ units

ear = ____ + ____ + ____ = ☐ units

ear = ____ + ____ + ____ = ☐ units

tail = ____ + ____ + ____ + ____ + ____ + ____ + ____ + ____ = ☐ units

B.

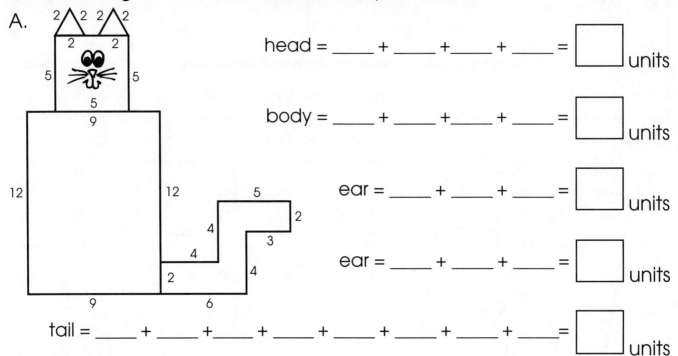

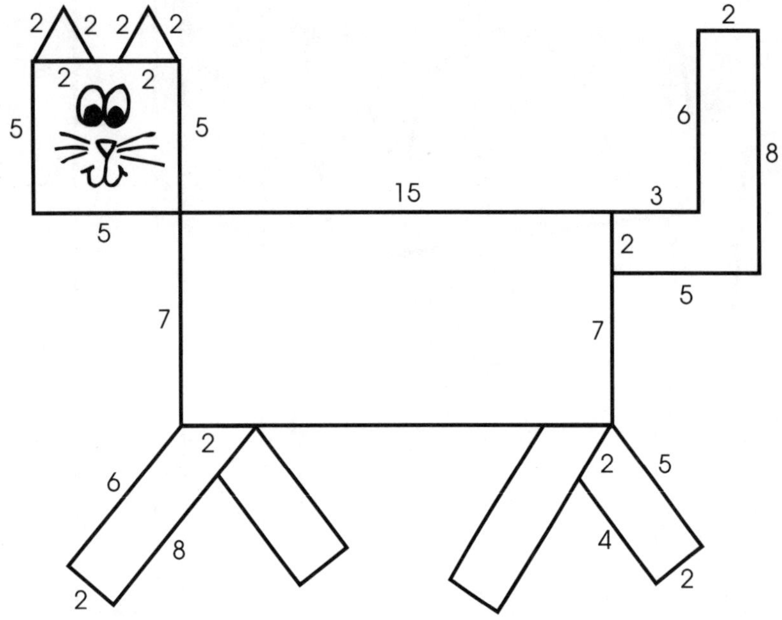

head = ☐ units

ears = ☐ units

body = ☐ units

tail = ☐ units

front leg = ☐ units

back leg = ☐ units

Name

Predicting patterns

Unit 3

Patterns are repeating, or continuing, pictures or numbers that can be predicted.

Continue each pattern by drawing three more pictures.

A.

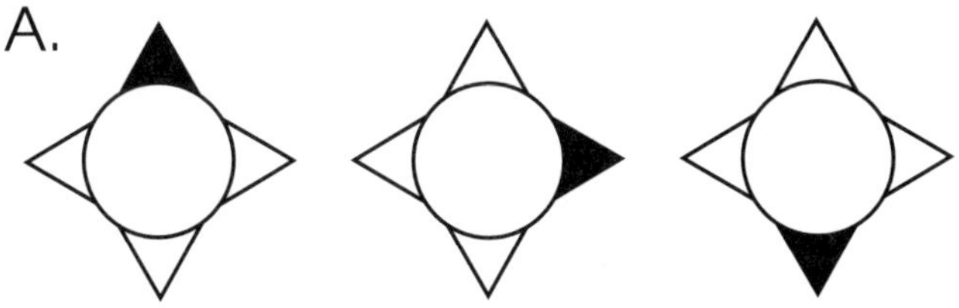

B.

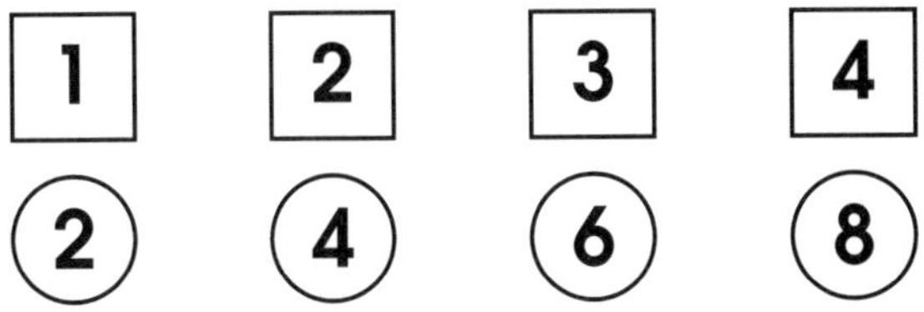

C.

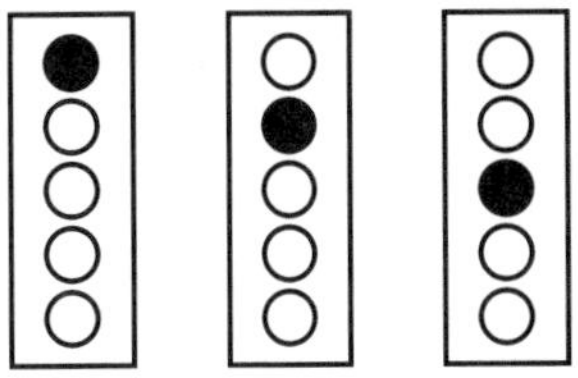

D.

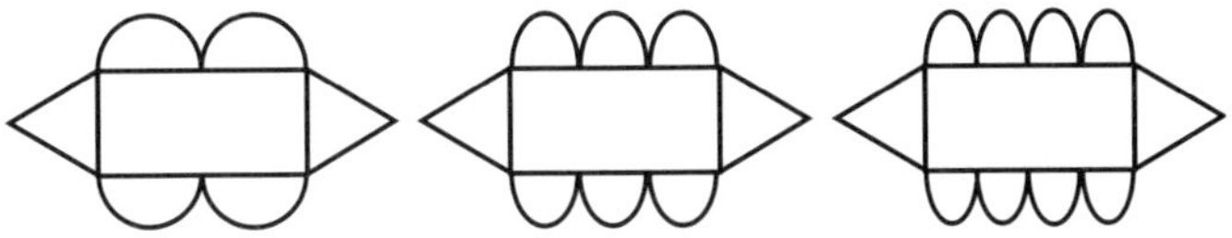

E.

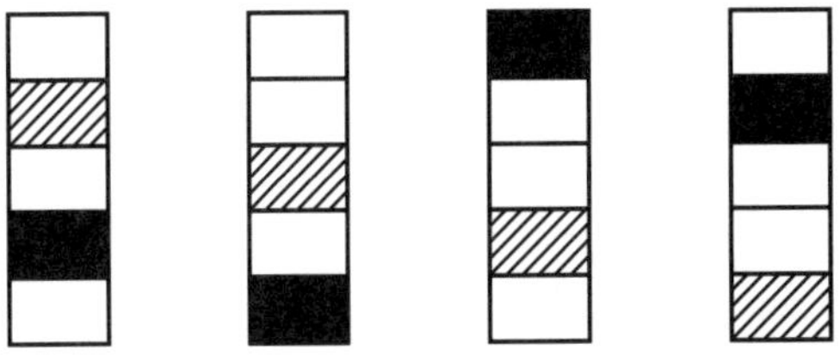

F.

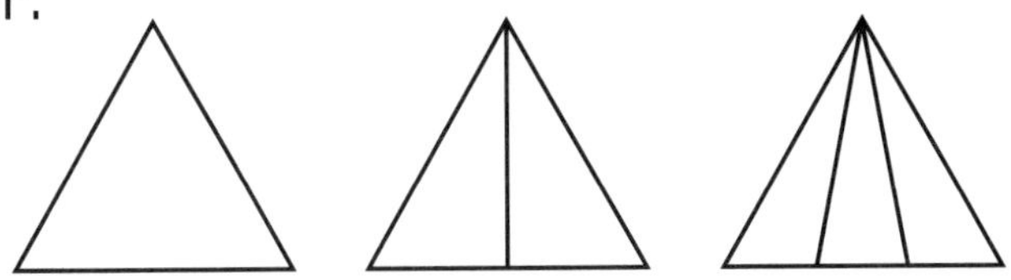

Name

Unit 3 Test

Page 1

Geometry

Read or listen to the question. Fill in the circle beside the best answer.

❑ Example:
Look at the groups of lines. Which one can be used to make a square?

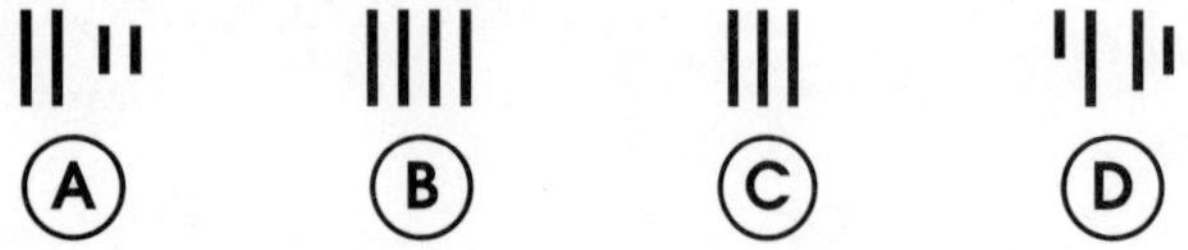

Answer: B because a square has four equal sides.

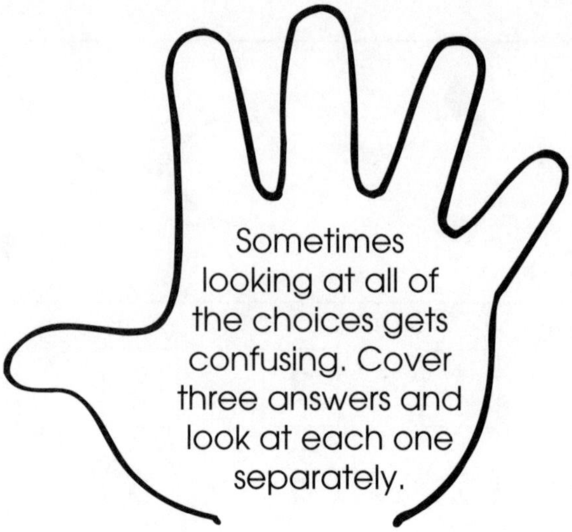

Sometimes looking at all of the choices gets confusing. Cover three answers and look at each one separately.

Now try these. You have 20 minutes.

Continue until you see STOP.

1. Which of these pictures shows an oval in a rectangle?

2. How many cylinders are there?

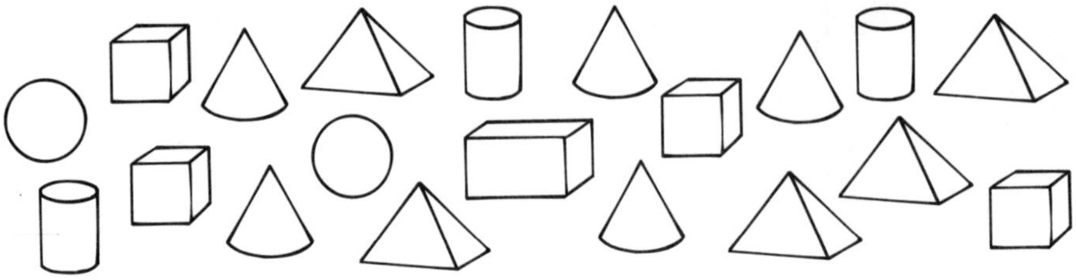

Ⓐ 3
Ⓑ 4
Ⓒ 2
Ⓓ 0

GO ON

Name

Unit 3 Test

Page 2

3. Which shape **does not** have four endpoints?

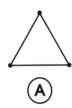

(A) (B) (C) (D)

4. Which figure **is not** like the others?

(A) (B) (C) (D)

5. Which figure is the same size and shape as Figure 1?

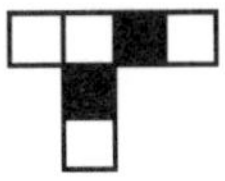

Figure 1

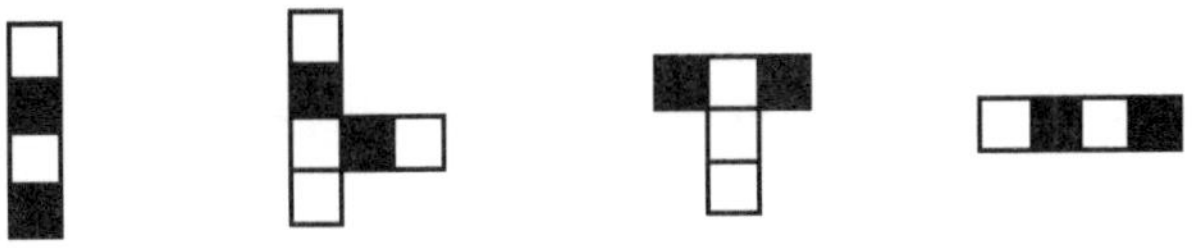

(A) (B) (C) (D)

6. Which figure could be folded on the dotted line to make the two sides match exactly?

(A) (B) (C) (D)

7. What is the perimeter of this figure?

16	15	12	10
(A)	(B)	(C)	(D)

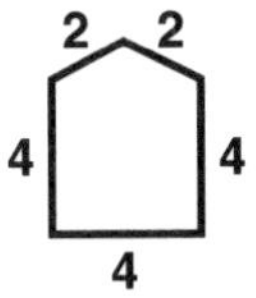

GO ON

Name

Unit 3 Test

8. Complete the pattern.

(A)  (B) 

(C)  (D) 

9. Find the answer to the riddle.
I am a number that is not in the rectangle or the triangle.
What number am I?

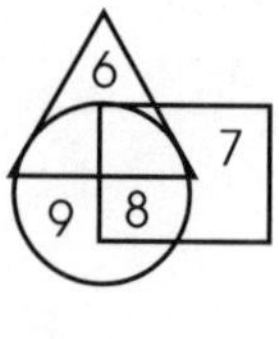

(A) 6 (B) 7

(C) 8 (D) 9

10. What is the perimeter of this square?

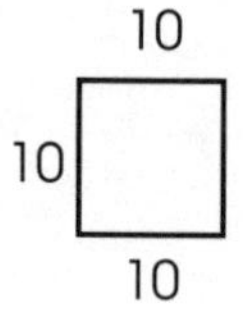

40 (A) 30 (B) 20 (C) 10 (D)

11. Which group has the most cubes?

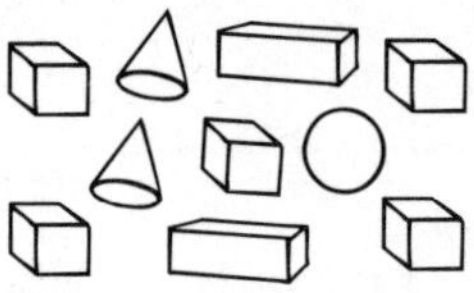 (A)

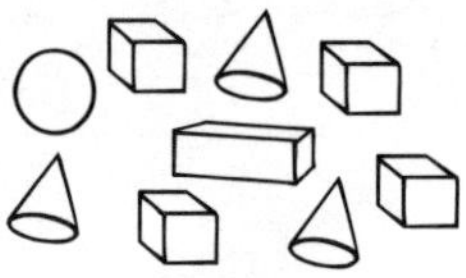 (B)

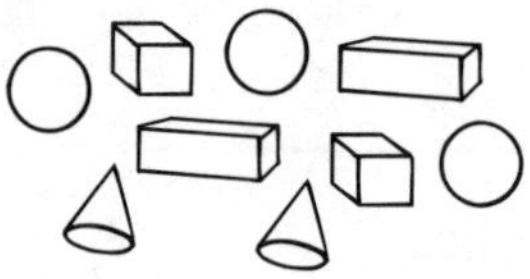 (C)

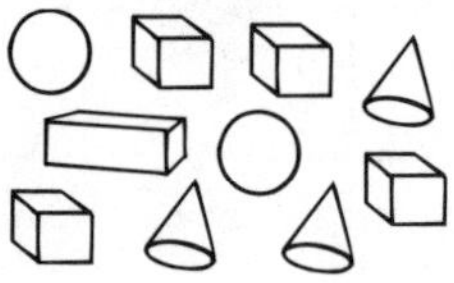 (D)

12. Which shape has the same number of line segments as Figure 1?

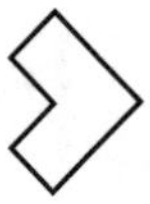

Figure 1

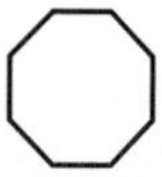 (A)

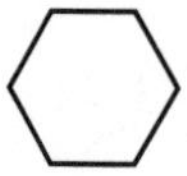 (B)

 (C)

 (D)

GO ON

Name

Unit 3 Test

13. Which piece is missing from the puzzle?

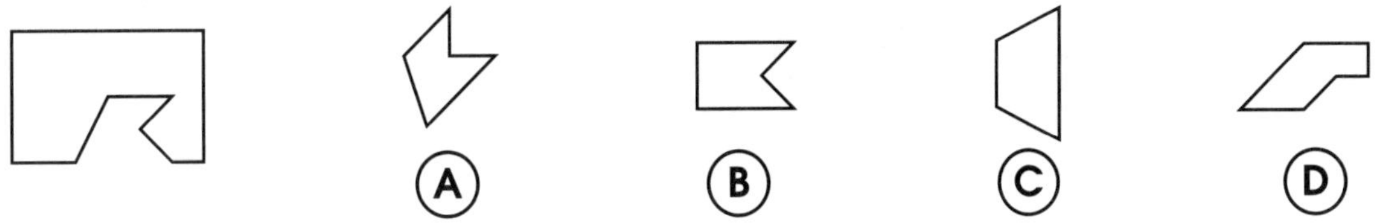

14. Which picture shows the rotation of Figure 1?

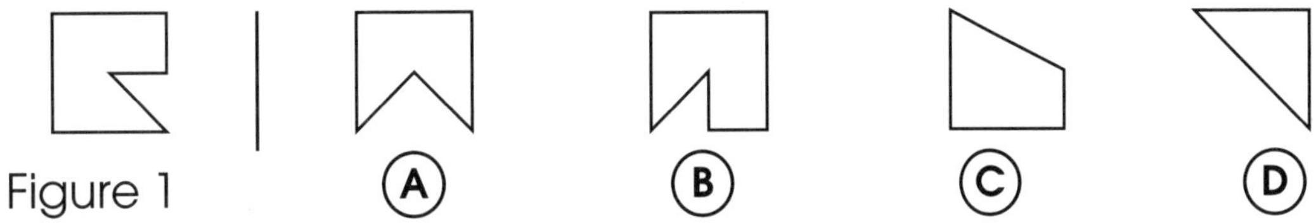

15. Figure 1 shows half of Anna's picture. Mark the other half.

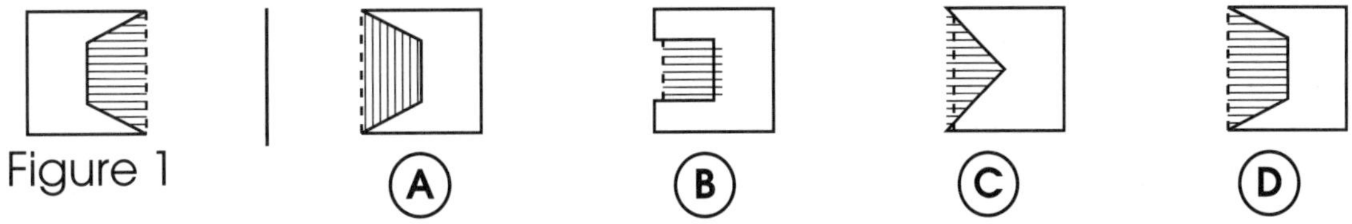

16. Complete the pattern.

17. Look at the lines in each group. Which group of lines could be used to make a rectangle?

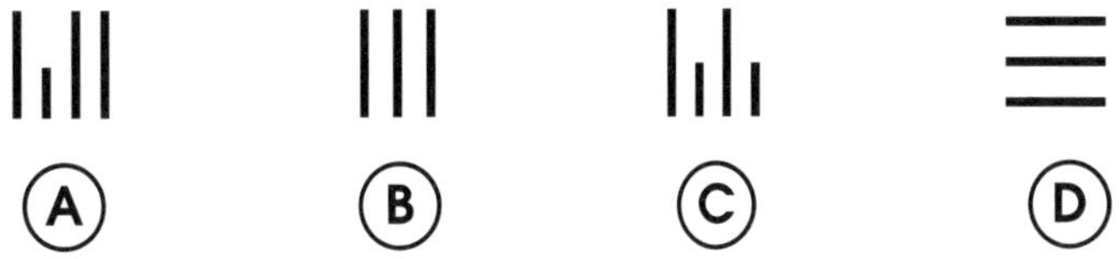

GO ON

Name

Unit 3 Test

Page 5

18. Look at the figures in the box. How many figures have 3 angles?

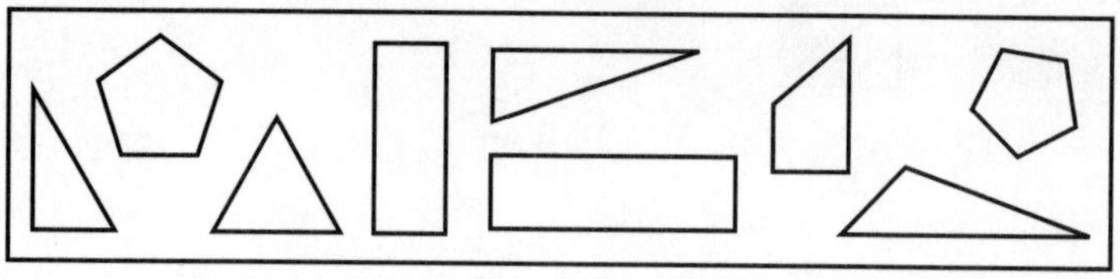

Ⓐ 2

Ⓑ 3

Ⓒ 4

Ⓓ 5

19. Which picture shows a line of symmetry?

Ⓐ

Ⓑ

Ⓒ

Ⓓ

20. Which figure is not like the others?

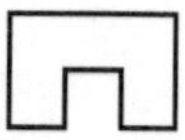

Ⓐ

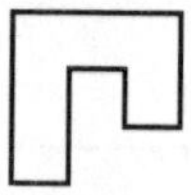

Ⓑ

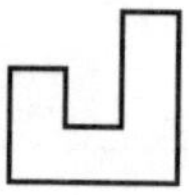

Ⓒ

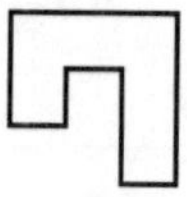

Ⓓ

Draw a shape with 6 points and 6 line segments.

STOP

Name

Adding basic facts

Unit 4

Addition facts are problems with 1-digit addends that you can memorize. They start at 0 + 0 and go up to 9 + 9.

Answer each fact. Color the magnifying glasses with even numbered answers to make a path to the ants.

9 + 5 = ____

4 + 8 = ____

6 + 7 = ____

5 + 8 = ____

8 + 8 = ____

6 + 3 = ____

9 + 8 = ____

5 + 7 = ____

9 + 7 = ____

8 + 5 = ____

6 + 4 = ____

7 + 8 = ____

7 + 7 = ____

8 + 3 = ____

6 + 9 = ____

9 + 9 = ____

9 + 4 = ____

Name

Adding basic facts/commutative property

Unit 4

Each part of an addition problem has a name. The numbers being added are called addends and the answer is called the sum. They form a number sentence. The addends can be switched around, and the sum stays the same! This is called the commutative property of addition.

Example: $8 + 7 = 15$ $7 + 8 = 15$ So . . . $8 + 7 = 7 + 8$

addend sum

Fill in the missing addends and sums.

A.

$6 + \boxed{} = 10$

$\boxed{} + 7 = 14$

$8 + \boxed{} = 16$

$\boxed{} + 5 = 10$

$7 + \boxed{} = 13$

$\boxed{} + 9 = 17$

B.

$5 + \boxed{} = 13$

$\boxed{} + 9 = 18$

$4 + \boxed{} = 11$

$\boxed{} + 8 = 14$

$6 + \boxed{} = 12$

$\boxed{} + 8 = 11$

C.

$7 + \boxed{} = 12$

$\boxed{} + 8 = 17$

$9 + \boxed{} = 15$

$\boxed{} + 7 = 16$

$9 + \boxed{} = 14$

$\boxed{} + 7 = 15$

D.

$8 + 7 = \boxed{} + 8$

$6 + \boxed{} = 9 + 6$

$\boxed{} + 5 = 5 + 9$

$7 + 6 = 6 + \boxed{}$

Adding 2- and 3-digit numbers with no regrouping — Unit 4

To find the sum of 2-digit numbers, always add the ones column first. Then add the tens column.

T	O
3	6
+ 2	3
	9

then

T	O
3	6
+ 2	3
5	9

To find the sum of 3-digit numbers, again add the ones column first. Then add the tens column, and last, add the hundreds column.

H	T	O
4	1	5
+ 3	8	2
		7

then

H	T	O
4	1	5
+ 3	8	2
	9	7

then

H	T	O
4	1	5
+ 3	8	2
7	9	7

Who has the most money? Find each sum, and then color the answers on the piggy banks. The first bank to be completely colored is the winner.

A.
```
   516        641        523        602
 +  22      + 341      + 311      + 135
```

B.
```
              221        414        496
            + 425      + 315      + 500
```

C.
```
   814        581        623        203
 +  72      + 102      + 311      + 272
```

475	982
834	683
729	886

934	996
737	538

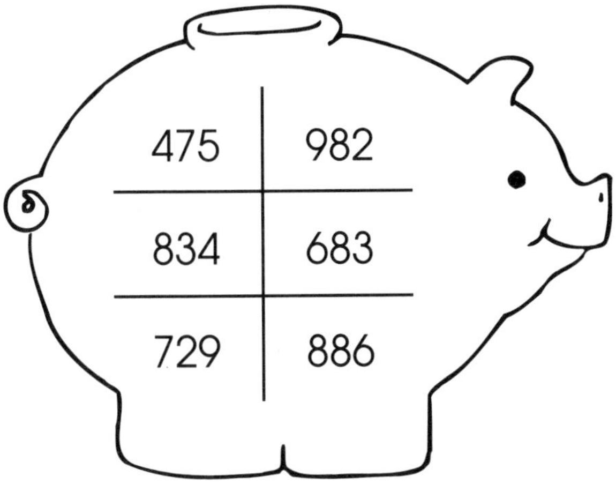

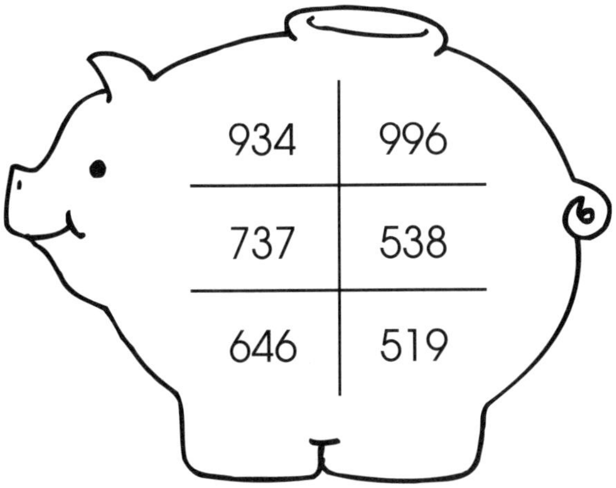

Name

Adding without regrouping/greater than, less than

Unit 4

Which is greater? 35 or 58? Your answer can be written using one of these symbols:

 ‹ means less than › means greater than

Example: 35 ‹ 58 or 58 › 35

Answer each problem. Then write **<** or **>** to compare the sums.

```
      213          372        A.    28          36
    + 450        + 614            + 51        + 41
   ───────  <   ───────          ─────  ◯   ─────
     663          986
```

```
 B.   485          324        C.   111         546
    + 114        + 201            +  74       + 201
    ─────  ◯    ─────            ─────  ◯   ─────
```

```
 D.   405          311        E.   402         612
    + 252        + 665            + 417       + 281
    ─────  ◯    ─────            ─────  ◯   ─────
```

```
 F.   533          421        G.    78          30
    + 266        + 341            +  11       +  50
    ─────  ◯    ─────            ─────  ◯   ─────
```

```
 H.   409          356        I.   520         273
    +  90        + 231            + 307       + 514
    ─────  ◯    ─────            ─────  ◯   ─────
```

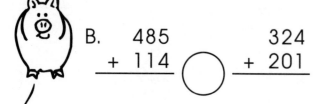

Name

Regrouping from ones to tens

Unit 4

Look at the groups. Each picture shows more than ten one blocks. They need to be regrouped. This means trading 10 of the ones to make another ten.

Example:

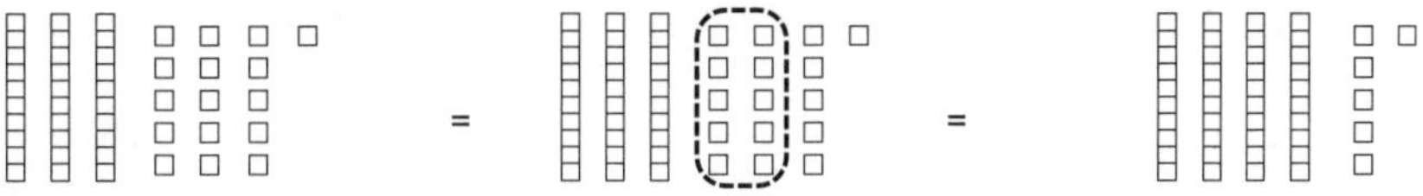

3 tens 16 ones = 4 tens 6 ones

Make another group of ten and write the number a new way.

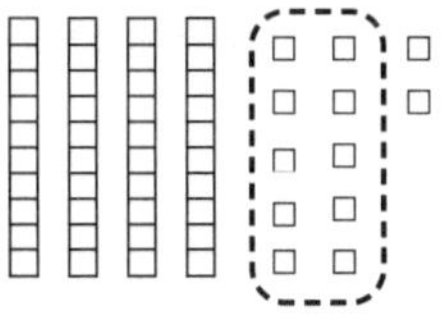

4 tens 12 ones

T	O
5	2

A. 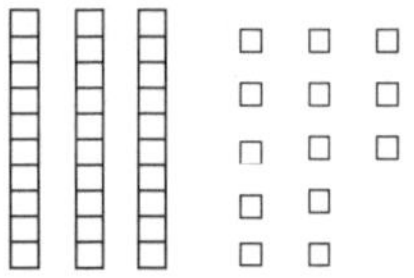

3 tens 13 ones

T	O

B. 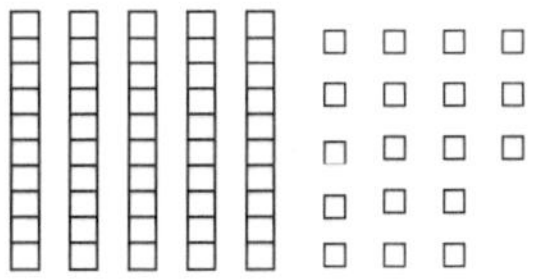

5 tens 18 ones

T	O

C. 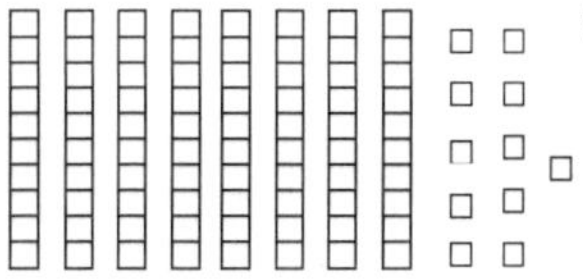

8 tens 11 ones

T	O

D. 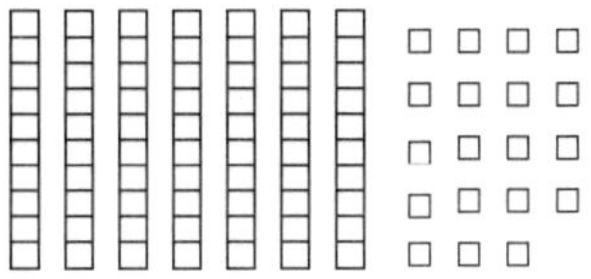

7 tens 19 ones

T	O

E. 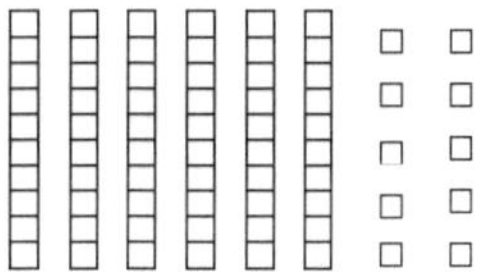

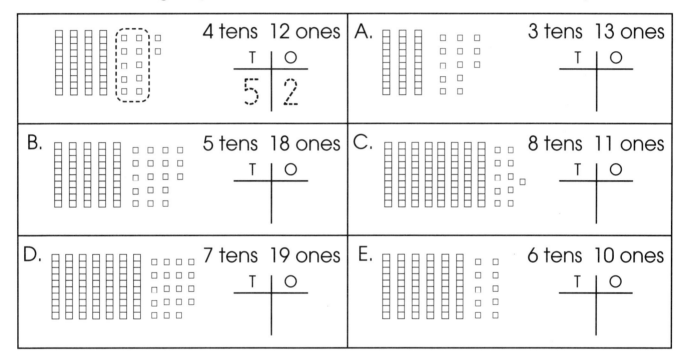

6 tens 10 ones

T	O

Now try it without pictures. Write the new number in the tens and ones columns.

F. 2 tens 11 ones

T	O

G. 7 tens 10 ones

T	O

H. 1 tens 18 ones

T	O

I. 6 tens 14 ones

T	O

J. 5 tens 19 ones

T	O

K. 8 tens 13 ones

T	O

Name

Adding 2-digit numbers regrouping

Unit 4

Sometimes when you are adding 2-digit numbers, the sum in the ones column is 10 or higher. Then you have to regroup to the tens column. Example:

$$\begin{array}{r|l} 2 & 8 \\ + \; 4 & 5 \\ \hline & \end{array}$$

8 + 5 = 13

Write the numbers in the columns as shown.

1. Add ones.

$$\begin{array}{r|l} 1 & \\ 2 & 8 \\ + \; 4 & 5 \\ \hline & 3 \end{array}$$

8 + 5 = 13 ones
13 ones = 1 ten 3 ones

2. Now add the tens column.

$$\begin{array}{r|l} 1 & \\ 2 & 8 \\ + \; 4 & 5 \\ \hline 7 & 3 \end{array}$$

Find the sums by regrouping.

A.

$$\begin{array}{r} 64 \\ +\ 18 \\ \hline \end{array} \qquad \begin{array}{r} 76 \\ +\ 15 \\ \hline \end{array} \qquad \begin{array}{r} 29 \\ +\ 42 \\ \hline \end{array} \qquad \begin{array}{r} 63 \\ +\ 29 \\ \hline \end{array}$$

B.

$$\begin{array}{r} 35 \\ +\ 36 \\ \hline \end{array} \qquad \begin{array}{r} 47 \\ +\ 28 \\ \hline \end{array} \qquad \begin{array}{r} 26 \\ +\ 16 \\ \hline \end{array} \qquad \begin{array}{r} 17 \\ +\ 25 \\ \hline \end{array}$$

C.

$$\begin{array}{r} 43 \\ +\ 27 \\ \hline \end{array} \qquad \begin{array}{r} 55 \\ +\ 35 \\ \hline \end{array} \qquad \begin{array}{r} 35 \\ +\ 59 \\ \hline \end{array} \qquad \begin{array}{r} 49 \\ +\ 39 \\ \hline \end{array}$$

D.

$$\begin{array}{r} 82 \\ +\ 9 \\ \hline \end{array} \qquad \begin{array}{r} 46 \\ +\ 17 \\ \hline \end{array} \qquad \begin{array}{r} 76 \\ +\ 18 \\ \hline \end{array} \qquad \begin{array}{r} 38 \\ +\ 38 \\ \hline \end{array}$$

Name

Adding 3-digit numbers regrouping from ones to tens

Unit 4

Sometimes when you are adding 3-digit numbers, the sum in the ones column will be 10 or higher. Then you have to regroup to the tens column. Example:

1. Add ones.

```
    3|2|8
+   2|4|7
```

8 + 7 = 15 ones
15 ones = 1 ten 5 ones

2. Regroup.

```
      1
    3|2|8
+   2|4|7
        5
```

3. Now add the tens and hundreds.

```
      1
    3|2|8
+   2|4|7
    5|7|5
```

Find each sum by regrouping. Then use the code to answer the riddle.

What cake is as hard as a rock?

____ ____ ____ ____ ____ ____
888 591 674 575 492 923

____ ____ ____ ____ !
796 591 960 923

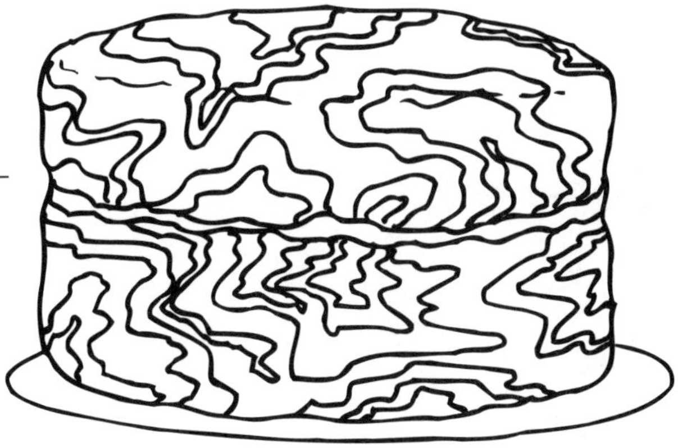

R 245 + 429	**E** 617 + 306	**K** 532 + 428	**B** 546 + 29
L 385 + 107	**S** 218 + 145	**M** 439 + 449	**D** 374 + 206
V 708 + 59	**A** 275 + 316	**P** 137 + 507	**C** 268 + 528

Name

Adding 3-digit numbers regrouping from tens to hundreds

Unit 4

Sometimes when you are adding 3-digit numbers, the sum in the tens column will be 10 or higher. Regrouping from the tens to the hundreds works the same way as regrouping from the ones to the tens. Example:

1. Add ones.

	4	3	2
+	3	8	1
			3

2. Add tens.

	4	3	2
+	3	8	1
			3

3 + 8 = 11 tens
11 tens =
1 hundred 1 ten

3. Regroup.

	1		
	4	3	2
+	3	8	1
		1	3

4. Now add the hundreds.

	1		
	4	3	2
+	3	8	1
	8	1	3

Find the sums by regrouping.

A.

491	346	242	489
+ 454	+ 192	+ 271	+ 340

B.

287	458	664	375
+ 191	+ 351	+ 273	+ 332

C.

193	674	560	293
+ 95	+ 185	+ 80	+ 361

Write a 3-digit addition problem showing regrouping from tens to hundreds. Find the sum.

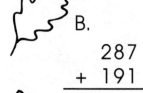

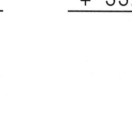

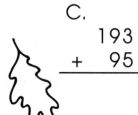

Name

Adding 3-digit numbers regrouping twice

Unit 4

Sometimes 3-digit addition problems need to be regrouped twice. Example:

1. Add ones.

$$\begin{array}{r|r|r} & 3 & 5 & 8 \\ + & 2 & 7 & 6 \\ \hline & & & \end{array}$$

8 + 6 = 14 ones
14 ones = 1 ten 4 ones

2. Regroup. Then add the tens.

$$\begin{array}{rr|r|r} & & 1 & \\ & 3 & 5 & 8 \\ + & 2 & 7 & 6 \\ \hline & & & 4 \end{array}$$

3. Regroup. Then add the hundreds.

$$\begin{array}{rr|r|r} & 1 & 1 & \\ & 3 & 5 & 8 \\ + & 2 & 7 & 6 \\ \hline & 6 & 3 & 4 \end{array}$$

Find the sums by regrouping.

A.

794	458	388	271
+ 126	+ 263	+ 364	+ 649

B.

536	265	429	698
+ 397	+ 138	+ 392	+ 258

C.

668	715	287	399
+ 194	+ 196	+ 529	+ 343

D.

458	538	147	616
+ 194	+ 95	+ 585	+ 286

Name

Multiplication as repeated groups

Unit 4

The multiplication sign (x) means "groups of." 3 x 2 means 3 groups of 2.

Draw a line from the multiplication problem to its picture.

3 x 3

1 x 5

4 x 2

3 x 2

---

1 x 4

5 x 2

3 x 1

3 x 4

Name

Multiplication as repeated addition

Unit 4

To find the answer to a multiplication problem, add all of the groups together. The answer is called the product.

Example: 3 x 2 = ★★ ★★ ★★ = 2 + 2 + 2 = 6
(3 groups of 2)

Draw groups to match the multiplication problem. Add the groups together. Then find the product.

A. 4 x 2 =	=	=	☐
B. 3 x 3 =	=	=	☐
C. 3 x 4 =	=	=	☐
D. 2 x 6 =	=	=	☐
E. 2 x 2 =	=	=	☐
F. 2 x 5 =	=	=	☐
G. 4 x 1 =	=	=	☐

Name

Unit 4 Test

Addition Computation

Read or listen to the question. Use an extra piece of paper to solve the problems. Fill in the circle beside the best answer.

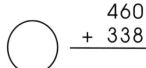

Find your own answer before you look at the choices.

❑ Example:

Find the sum.

$$\begin{array}{r} 349 \\ +\ 229 \\ \hline \end{array}$$

(A) 568
(B) 678
(C) 569
(D) 578

Answer: D because the correct answer is 578.

Now try these. You have 20 minutes. Continue until you see STOP.

1. Which number sentence does not equal 15?

$7 + 8 = \square$	$9 + 6 = \square$	$7 + 7 = \square$	$5 + 10 = \square$
(A)	(B)	(C)	(D)

2.

$$\begin{array}{r} 236 \\ +\ 423 \\ \hline \end{array}$$

569	659	668	649
(A)	(B)	(C)	(D)

3. Which number sentence matches the sums to this problem?

$$\begin{array}{r} 342 \\ +\ 353 \\ \hline \end{array} \quad \bigcirc \quad \begin{array}{r} 460 \\ +\ 338 \\ \hline \end{array}$$

$695 < 798$	$695 > 798$	$965 < 798$	$695 < 789$
(A)	(B)	(C)	(D)

GO ON

Name

Unit 4 Test

4. Which number shows regrouping 3 tens 19 ones?

(A)

T	O
9	3

(B)

T	O
10	9

(C)

T	O
	3

(D)

T	O
4	9

5. 67 + 18

(A) 75 (B) 58 (C) 85 (D) 68

6. 382 + 459

(A) 731 (B) 841 (C) 741 (D) 832

7. 55¢ + 34¢

(A) 59¢ (B) 35¢ (C) 98¢ (D) 89¢

8. Mark the number sentence that matches the picture.

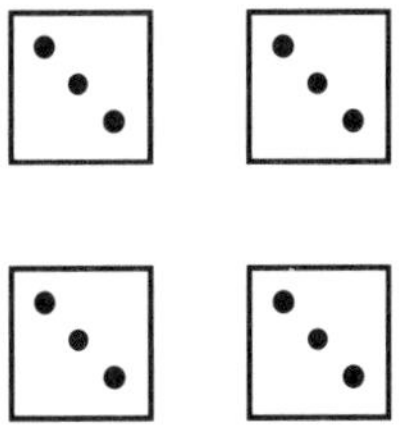

(A) $4 \times 3 = 12$
(B) $4 + 3 = 7$
(C) $4 < 12$
(D) $2 + 2 = 4$

9. 359 + 306

(A) 556 (B) 605 (C) 665 (D) 656

GO ON

Name

Unit 4 Test

10. Mark the fact that matches the picture.

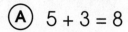

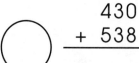

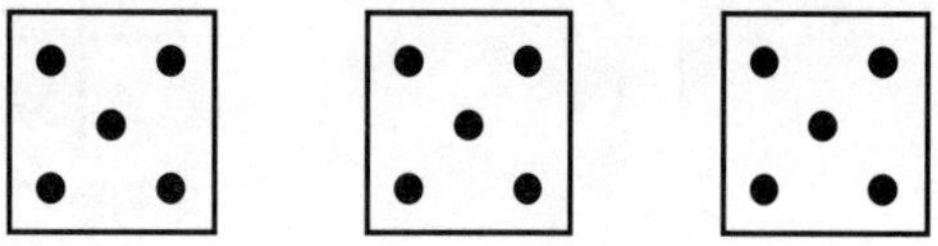

(A) $5 + 3 = 8$

(B) $3 \times 3 = 9$

(C) $3 \times 5 = 15$

(D) $5 < 15$

11. Fill in the missing number. $21 + 14 = \square + 21$

(A) 21 (B) 11 (C) 4 (D) 14

12. Which number sentence matches the sums to this problem?

$$\begin{array}{r} 614 \\ +\ 302 \\ \hline \end{array} \quad \bigcirc \quad \begin{array}{r} 430 \\ +\ 538 \\ \hline \end{array}$$

(A) $916 < 968$ (B) $916 > 968$ (C) $906 < 958$ (D) $906 < 968$

13. Which number shows regrouping 6 tens 13 ones?

	T	O
(A)	6	3
(B)	7	3
(C)	3	6
(D)	4	9

14.

$$\begin{array}{r} 53 \\ +\ 27 \\ \hline \end{array}$$

(A) 70 (B) 80 (C) 90 (D) 79

15.

$$\begin{array}{r} 563 \\ +\ 164 \\ \hline \end{array}$$

(A) 607 (B) 667 (C) 727 (D) 627

GO ON

Name

Unit 4 Test

16. What is the missing addend in this addition sentence?

5 + ☐ = 13

Ⓐ 8 Ⓑ 7 Ⓒ 6 Ⓓ 9

17. How many of these facts equal 12?

$$\begin{array}{r} 6 \\ +\ 6 \\ \hline \end{array} \quad \begin{array}{r} 5 \\ +\ 5 \\ \hline \end{array} \quad \begin{array}{r} 7 \\ +\ 3 \\ \hline \end{array} \quad \begin{array}{r} 5 \\ +\ 7 \\ \hline \end{array} \quad \begin{array}{r} 9 \\ +\ 3 \\ \hline \end{array}$$

Ⓐ 2 Ⓑ 3 Ⓒ 4 Ⓓ 1

18. Mark the multiplication sentence that matches the picture.

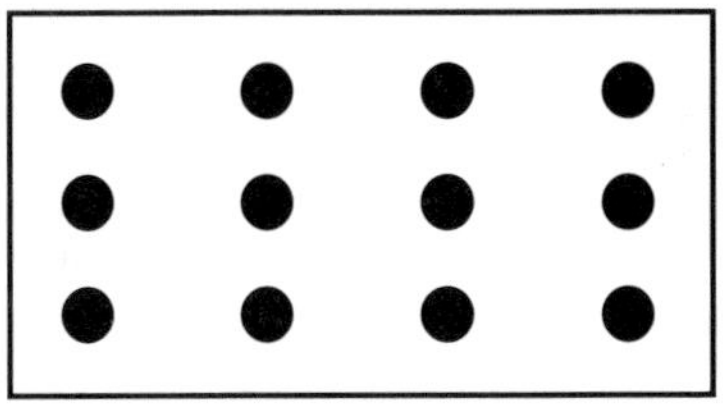

Ⓐ 1 x 4 = 4

Ⓑ 3 x 3 = 9

Ⓒ 4 x 4 = 16

Ⓓ 3 x 4 = 12

19.

$$\begin{array}{r} 914 \\ +\ \ 69 \\ \hline \end{array}$$

Ⓐ 970 Ⓑ 983 Ⓒ 907 Ⓓ 973

20.

$$\begin{array}{r} 498 \\ +\ 421 \\ \hline \end{array}$$

Ⓐ 919 Ⓑ 900 Ⓒ 909 Ⓓ 819

Write an addition problem. Use 2-digit numbers that need the ones regrouped. Find the sum.

STOP

Name

Midway Review Test

Page 1

Read or listen to the question. Use an extra piece of paper to solve the problems. Fill in the circle beside the best answer completely and neatly.

❑ Example:

Find the sum.

$$\begin{array}{r} 35 \\ +\ 37 \\ \hline \end{array}$$

Ⓐ 62 Ⓑ 70

Ⓒ 72 Ⓓ 61

Answer: C because the ones place totals 12, and you must regroup to the tens. Then add the tens.

Now try these. You have 25 minutes.

Continue until you see STOP.

Remember your Helping Hand Strategies:

1. Read all of the choices before you answer.

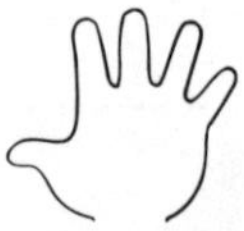
2. Cross out answers you know are wrong.

3. Sometimes looking at all of the choices gets confusing. Cover three answers and look at each one separately.

4. Find your own answer before you look at the choices.

1. Show the picture with 10 more than 45.

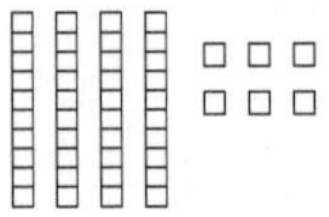
Ⓐ

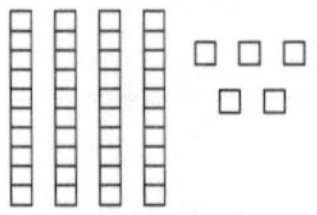
Ⓑ

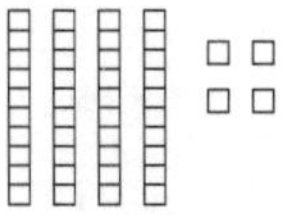
Ⓒ

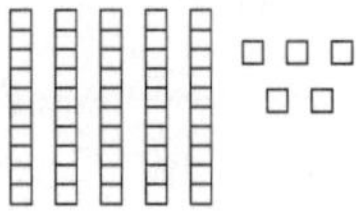
Ⓓ

2. Which number is the least?

400 + 20 + 1 Ⓐ

four hundred sixteen Ⓑ

4 hundreds, 3 tens, 2 ones Ⓒ

H	T	O
4	8	9

Ⓓ

GO ON

Name

Midway Review Test

Page 2

3. How many triangles inside ovals are shown?

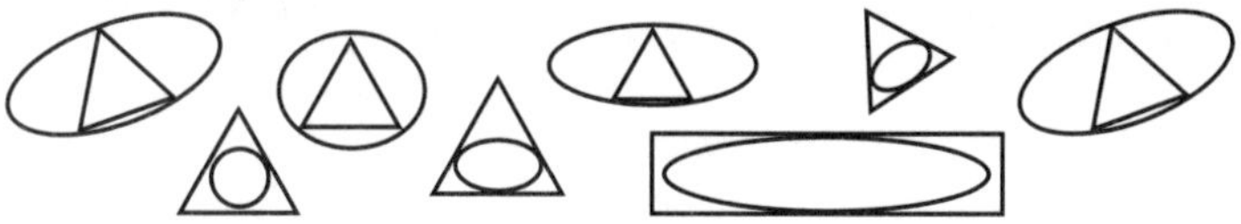

Ⓐ 1 Ⓑ 2 Ⓒ 3 Ⓓ 4

4. $\begin{array}{r} 654 \\ +\ 127 \\ \hline \end{array}$

871 Ⓐ 771 Ⓑ 781 Ⓒ 881 Ⓓ

5. Solve the riddle.

I can be rounded to 90. I am an odd number. My digits add up to 13. Who am I?

Ⓐ 87 Ⓑ 85 Ⓒ 83 Ⓓ 91

6. What is the perimeter of the rectangle?

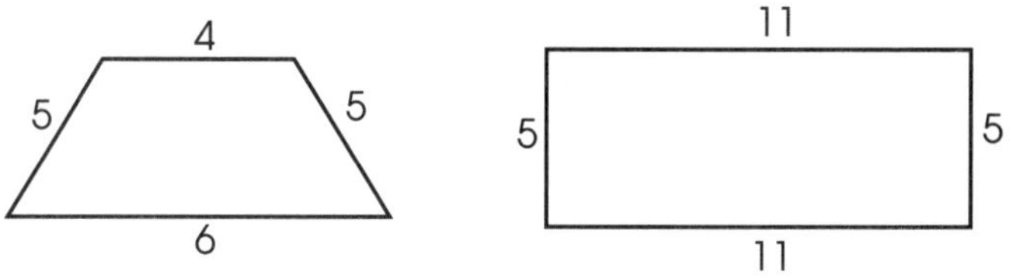

Ⓐ 20
Ⓑ 28
Ⓒ 32
Ⓓ 24

7. Mark the fact that matches the picture.

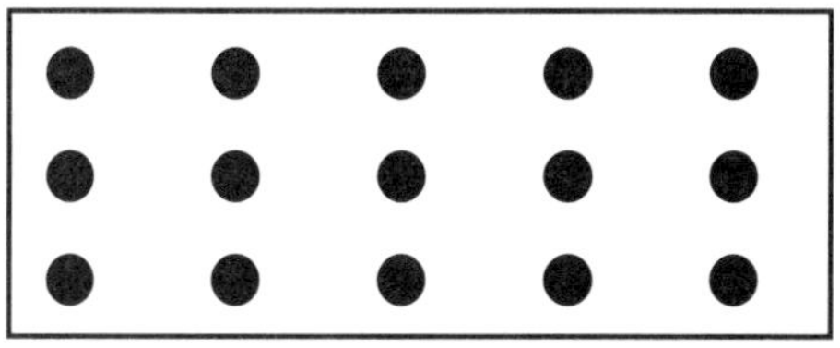

Ⓐ 3 x 5 = 15
Ⓑ 3 + 5 = 8
Ⓒ 3 x 6 = 18
Ⓓ 2 x 5 = 10

8. Round 489 to the nearest hundred.

400 Ⓐ 500 Ⓑ 600 Ⓒ 550 Ⓓ

GO ON

Name

Midway Review Test

9. What even number is in the triangle and rectangle, but not in the circle?

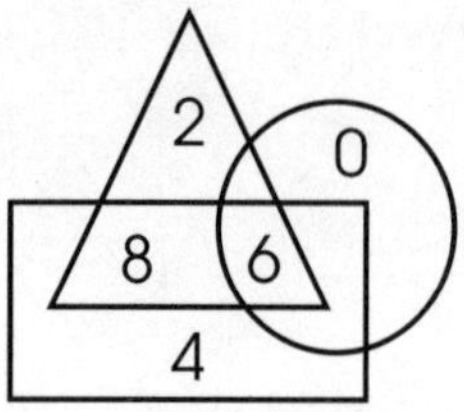

6 (A)   8 (B)   2 (C)   4 (D)

10. Finish the number line.

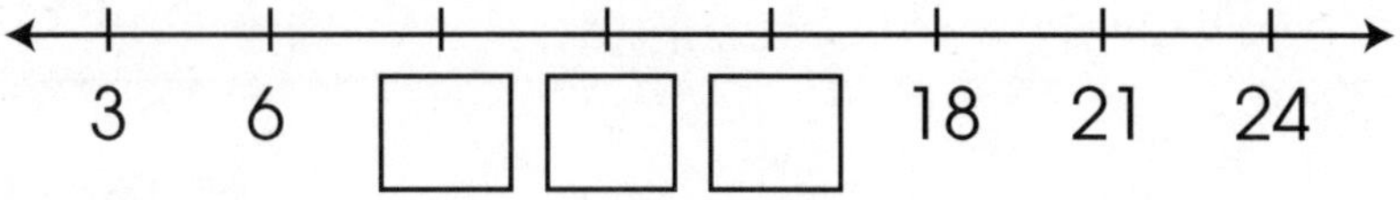

(A) 7, 8, 9
(B) 8, 10, 12
(C) 9, 12, 15
(D) 12, 15, 18

11. Complete the pattern.

(A)

(B)

(C)

(D)

12. Which number sentence matches the sums to this problem?

$$\begin{array}{r} 345 \\ +\ 211 \\ \hline \end{array} \quad \bigcirc \quad \begin{array}{r} 472 \\ +\ 109 \\ \hline \end{array}$$

$556 > 581$ (A) $556 < 581$ (B) $558 < 571$ (C) $576 > 591$ (D)

13. Which number is 10 less than 74?

60 + 4 (A)   70 + 4 (B)   40 + 7 (C)   40 + 6 (D)

GO ON

Name

Midway Review Test

14. How many miles is it to St. Louis?

(A) three hundred ninety-eight
(B) eight hundred thirty-nine
(C) three hundred eighty-nine
(D) eight hundred ninety-three

15. How many spheres are shown?

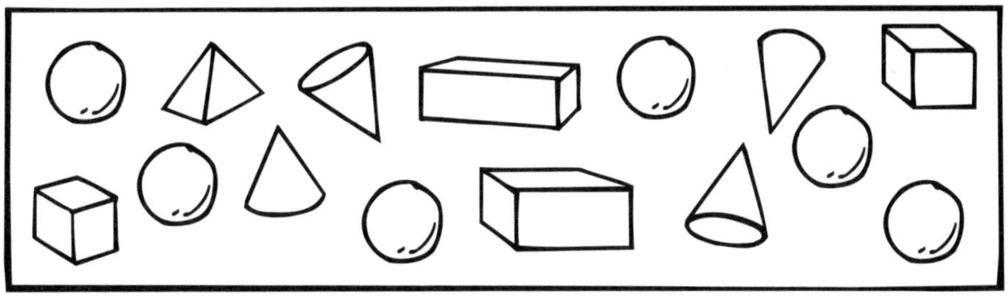

5	6	7	8
(A)	(B)	(C)	(D)

16.

$$\begin{array}{r} 479 \\ +\ 401 \\ \hline \end{array}$$

880	980	870	890
(A)	(B)	(C)	(D)

17. Which number shows regrouping 5 tens 19 ones?

T | O	T | O	T | O	T | O
7 | 9	5 | 9	4 | 9	6 | 9
(A)	(B)	(C)	(D)

18. Which book has the most pages?

(A)

(B)

(C)

(D)

GO ON

Name

Midway Review Test

19. Which fish is fifth from the seaweed?

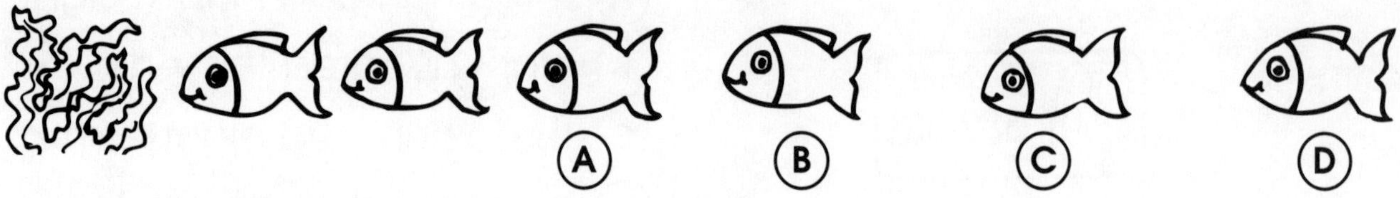

20. Which piece is missing from the puzzle?

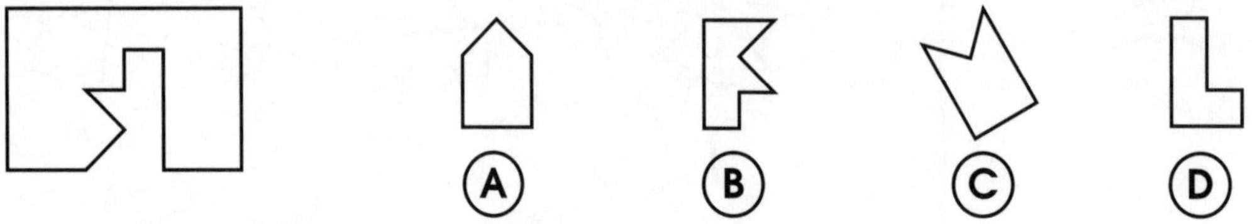

Write an addition problem with 3-digit numbers. Find the sum.

Name

Subtracting basic facts through 12

Unit 5

Subtraction facts are 1-digit problems that you can memorize. The answers to subtraction problems are called differences.

Which super hero will have a colored cape and fly the fastest? To find the real hero, color one part of the cape for each answer.

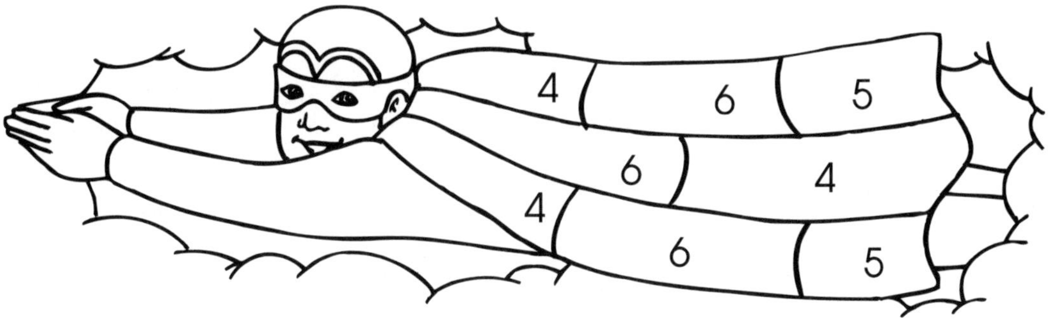

A. 10 – 5 = ______ 12 – 6 = ______ 10 – 7 = ______

B. 10 – 2 = ______ 11 – 4 = ______ 12 – 8 = ______

C. 11 – 8 = ______ 12 – 5 = ______ 10 – 6 = ______

D. 12 – 4 = ______ 12 – 7 = ______ 12 – 8 = ______

E. 12 – 3 = ______ 10 – 4 = ______ 11 – 2 = ______

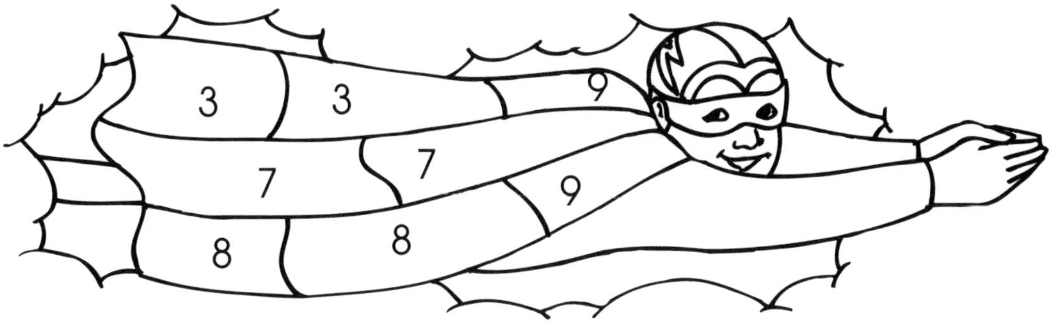

Name

Subtracting basic facts through 18 — Unit 5

If you can not remember a basic fact, use similar facts that you know to help you.

Follow the instructions at the top of each box to complete the fact tables.

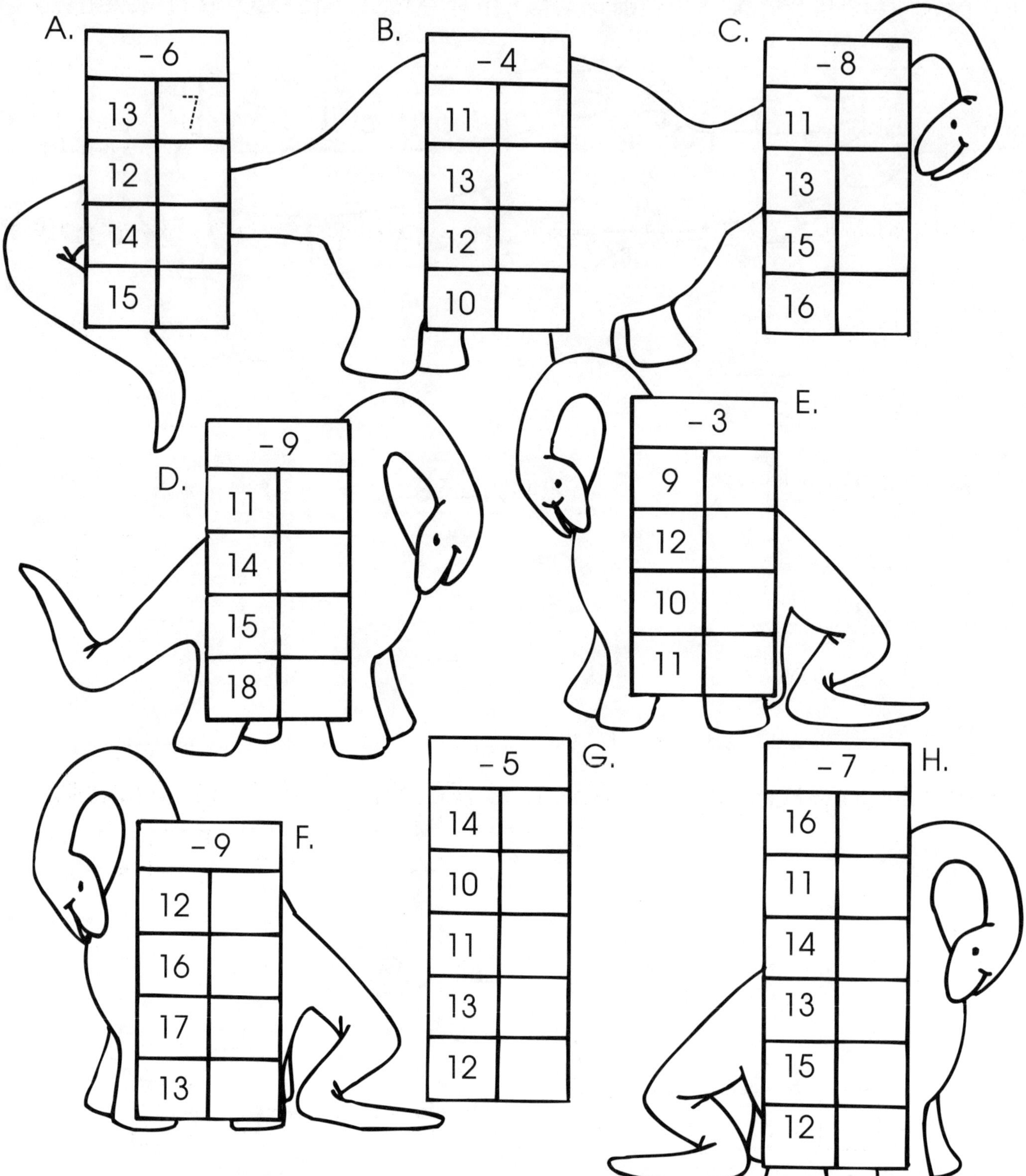

A.

− 6	
13	7
12	
14	
15	

B.

− 4	
11	
13	
12	
10	

C.

− 8	
11	
13	
15	
16	

D.

− 9	
11	
14	
15	
18	

E.

− 3	
9	
12	
10	
11	

F.

− 9	
12	
16	
17	
13	

G.

− 5	
14	
10	
11	
13	
12	

H.

− 7	
16	
11	
14	
13	
15	
12	

Name

Fact families

Unit 5

Some addition and subtraction problems are related like families. They can make two addition and two subtraction problems using the same three numbers. Example:

5 6 11

5 + 6 = 11 11 − 5 = 6

6 + 5 = 11 11 − 6 = 5

Use basic facts to find the family's name and write it on their mailbox.

A. The Miller Family

4 + [7] = 11

[7] + 4 = 11

11 − 4 = [7]

11 − [7] = 4

B. The Jones Family

7 + [ ] = 13

[ ] + 7 = 13

13 − 7 = [ ]

13 − [ ] = 7

C. The Smith Family

9 + [ ] = 12

[ ] + 9 = 12

12 − 9 = [ ]

12 − [ ] = 9

D. The Moore Family

8 + [ ] = 13

[ ] + 8 = 13

13 − 8 = [ ]

13 − [ ] = 8

E. The Nelson Family

7 + [ ] = 16

[ ] + 7 = 16

16 − 7 = [ ]

16 − [ ] = 7

F. The Hall Family

8 + [ ] = 12

[ ] + 8 = 12

12 − 8 = [ ]

12 − [ ] = 8

Name

Subtracting 2- and 3-digit numbers no regrouping

Unit 5

To subtract 2- or 3-digit numbers, begin with the ones column, then move on to the tens, and finally the hundreds. Example:

1. Subtract ones.

	H	T	O
	4	8	6
–	2	7	1
			5

2. Subtract tens.

	H	T	O
	4	8	6
–	2	7	1
		1	5

3. Subtract hundreds.

	H	T	O
	4	8	6
–	2	7	1
	2	1	5

Find the differences.

A.	672 – 430	518 – 201	776 – 43	493 – 182
B.	963 – 243	814 – 413	586 – 72	491 – 290
C.	375 – 40	609 – 608	980 – 870	974 – 521

Name

Regrouping from tens to ones

Unit 5

Look at this picture. One group of ten is being regrouped for 10 ones. The total number of blocks does not change, but the number of tens and ones does. Example:

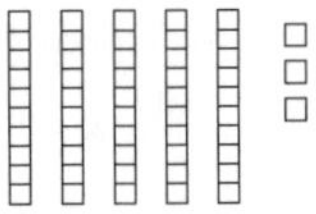

=

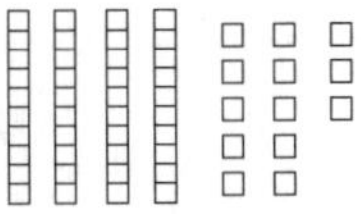

53 = 5 tens 3 ones = 4 tens 13 ones =

T	O
4	13
~~5~~	~~3~~

Regroup to make more ones.

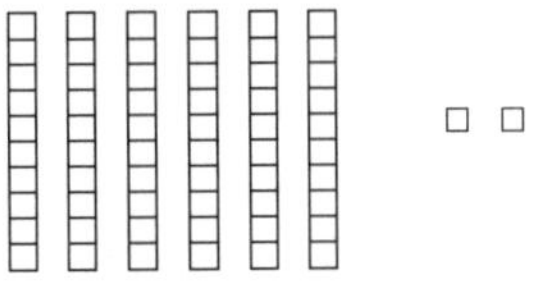

6 tens 2 ones =

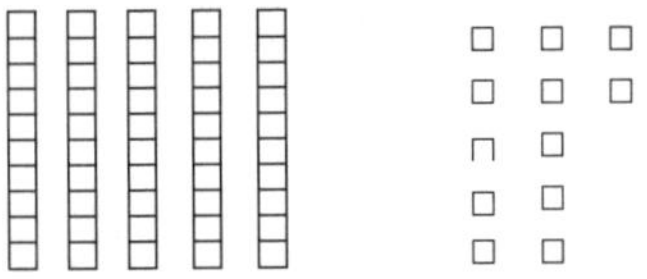

[5] tens [12] ones =

T	O
5	12
~~6~~	~~2~~

A.

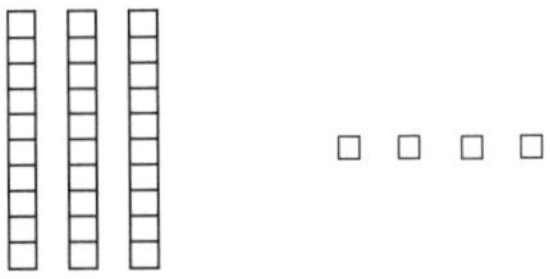

3 tens 4 ones =

[ ] tens [ ] ones =

T	O
3	4

Now try it without pictures. Regroup to make more ones.

B.

T	O
6	8

T	O
7	2

T	O
5	4

C.

T	O
9	6

T	O
6	0

T	O
8	4

D.

T	O
7	0

T	O
8	7

T	O
1	6

E.

T	O
1	2

T	O
2	0

T	O
4	3

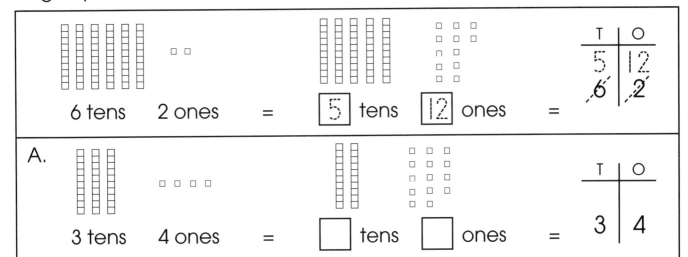

Name

Subtracting 2-digit numbers regrouping

Unit 5

Sometimes when subtracting, you must regroup before you can finish the problem.
Example:

1. Try to subtract ones.

```
  8 2
- 2 9
-----
```

I only have 2 ones!

2. Regroup.

```
  7 12
  8̸ 2̸
- 2  9
------
```

3. Subtract ones, then tens.

```
  7 12
  8̸ 2̸
- 2  9
------
  5  3
```

Find the differences by regrouping.

A.

64 − 18	52 − 16	94 − 36	81 − 74

B.

70 − 59	48 − 29	66 − 38	96 − 19

C.

41 − 27	84 − 36	80 − 64	78 − 9

Name

Subtracting 3-digit numbers regrouping from tens to ones

Unit 5

Regrouping from the tens to the ones works the same way with 3-digit numbers. Remember to start in the ones column.

1. Try to subtract ones.

```
  9 3 1
- 6 0 4
-------
```

I have only 1 one!

2. Regroup.

```
    2 11
  9 3̸ 1̸
- 6 0  4
--------
```

3. Subtract ones, tens, then hundreds.

```
    2 11
  9 3̸ 1̸
- 6 0  4
--------
  3 2  7
```

Find the differences by regrouping.

A.	230 − 117	456 − 127	843 − 418
B.	595 − 278	667 − 348	862 − 119
C.	550 − 428	782 − 549	690 − 145
D.	766 − 409	417 − 208	372 − 25

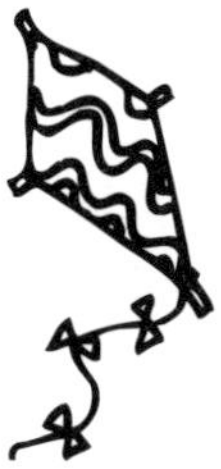

Name

Subtracting 3-digit numbers regrouping from hundreds to tens — Unit 5

With 3-digit numbers, you may need to regroup from the hundreds to the tens. It works the same way as when you regrouped from the tens to the ones. Example:

1. Try to subtract ones.	2. Try to subtract tens.		3. Regroup.	4. Subtract tens, then hundreds.
			5 12	5 12
6 2 9	6 2 9	I only	~~6~~ ~~2~~ 9	~~6~~ ~~2~~ 9
− 1 8 2	− 1 8 2	have	− 1 8 2	− 1 8 2
7	7	2 tens!	7	4 4 7

Find the differences by regrouping from the tens to the hundreds column.

A. $946 - 754$ $632 - 391$ $434 - 244$ $429 - 340$

B. $963 - 82$ $854 - 291$ $462 - 371$ $509 - 144$

C. $538 - 182$ $605 - 172$ $733 - 281$ $337 - 164$

Name

Subtracting 3-digit numbers regrouping twice

Unit 5

Sometimes 3-digit subtraction problems need to be regrouped twice. Example:

1. Try to subtract ones.

   $\begin{array}{r} 623 \\ -\ 145 \\ \hline \end{array}$ I only have 3 ones!

2. Regroup. Subtract ones.

   $\begin{array}{r} {}^{1\,13} \\ 6\not{2}\not{3} \\ -\ 145 \\ \hline 8 \end{array}$

3. Try to subtract tens.

   $\begin{array}{r} {}^{1\,13} \\ 6\not{2}\not{3} \\ -\ 145 \\ \hline 8 \end{array}$ I only have 1 ten!

4. Regroup. Subtract tens, then hundreds.

   $\begin{array}{r} {}^{5\,11\,13} \\ \not{6}\not{2}\not{3} \\ -\ 145 \\ \hline 478 \end{array}$

Find each difference. Then use the code to answer the joke.

What dance are the Pilgrims most known for?

___ ___ ___
395 267 558

___ ___ ___ ___ ___ ___ ___ ___
338 643 165 768 369 611 395 267

___ ___ ___ ___ !
739 369 189 484

P $\begin{array}{r} 621 \\ -\ 283 \\ \hline \end{array}$	**R** $\begin{array}{r} 917 \\ -\ 178 \\ \hline \end{array}$	**O** $\begin{array}{r} 438 \\ -\ 69 \\ \hline \end{array}$	**H** $\begin{array}{r} 553 \\ -\ 286 \\ \hline \end{array}$
M $\begin{array}{r} 941 \\ -\ 173 \\ \hline \end{array}$	**T** $\begin{array}{r} 864 \\ -\ 469 \\ \hline \end{array}$	**L** $\begin{array}{r} 740 \\ -\ 97 \\ \hline \end{array}$	**K** $\begin{array}{r} 982 \\ -\ 498 \\ \hline \end{array}$
E $\begin{array}{r} 616 \\ -\ 58 \\ \hline \end{array}$	**U** $\begin{array}{r} 804 \\ -\ 193 \\ \hline \end{array}$	**C** $\begin{array}{r} 464 \\ -\ 275 \\ \hline \end{array}$	**Y** $\begin{array}{r} 623 \\ -\ 458 \\ \hline \end{array}$

Name

Estimating/subtracting 3-digit numbers

Unit 5

To **estimate** means to make a close guess. To estimate these differences, round both numbers to the nearest hundred. Then subtract. Example:

298	→	Round to	300
− 72	→	Round to	− 100
			200 is the estimate!

Estimate the answers.

A. 864 →
− 328 → − ______

B. 716 →
− 152 → − ______

C. 924 →
− 376 → − ______

D. 298 →
− 173 → − ______

E. 415 →
− 392 → − ______

F. 649 →
− 193 → − ______

G. 762 →
− 248 → − ______

H. 803 →
− 461 → − ______

Write a 3-digit subtraction problem regrouping from tens to ones. Estimate the answer. Then find the difference.

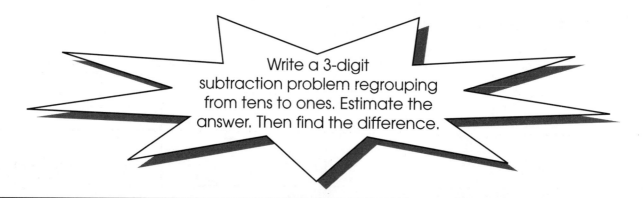

Name

Unit 5 Test

Page 1

Subtraction Computation

Read or listen to the question. Use an extra piece of paper to solve the problems. Fill in the circle beside the best answer.

When using scratch paper, copy carefully.

Example:

☐ Find the difference.

$$\begin{array}{r} 827 \\ -\ 574 \\ \hline \end{array}$$

Ⓐ 253

Ⓑ 353

Ⓒ 223

Ⓓ 323

Answer: A because the difference is 253.

Now try these. You have 20 minutes. Continue until you see STOP.

1. Which number will make both sentences true?

$\square + 8 = 15$

$15 - \square = 8$

9	7	6	8
Ⓐ	Ⓑ	Ⓒ	Ⓓ

2.

$$\begin{array}{r} 694 \\ -\ 301 \\ \hline \end{array}$$

293	691	303	393
Ⓐ	Ⓑ	Ⓒ	Ⓓ

3. Which number shows correct regrouping?

9 10 ~~90~~	10 10 ~~90~~	8 10 ~~90~~	9 1 ~~90~~
Ⓐ	Ⓑ	Ⓒ	Ⓓ

GO ON

Name

Unit 5 Test

Page 2

4.

$$\begin{array}{r} 82 \\ -\ 16 \\ \hline \end{array}$$

(A)	(B)	(C)	(D)
66	56	74	64

5. What sign is missing?

13 ☐ 7 = 6

(A)	(B)	(C)	(D)
+	–	x	<

6.

$$\begin{array}{r} 364 \\ -\ 117 \\ \hline \end{array}$$

(A)	(B)	(C)	(D)
253	257	247	243

7. Which number is missing?

8 + ☐ = 14

14 – ☐ = 8

(A)	(B)	(C)	(D)
9	7	6	8

8.

$$\begin{array}{r} 417 \\ -\ 142 \\ \hline \end{array}$$

(A)	(B)	(C)	(D)
275	335	559	375

9.

$$\begin{array}{r} 736 \\ -\ 197 \\ \hline \end{array}$$

(A)	(B)	(C)	(D)
661	639	549	539

10. Which is the best estimate?

$$\begin{array}{r} 936 \\ -\ 689 \\ \hline \end{array}$$

(A)	(B)	(C)	(D)
200	300	400	500

GO ON

Name

Unit 5 Test

11.

$$\begin{array}{r} 70 \\ -\ 48 \\ \hline \end{array}$$

Ⓐ 32 Ⓑ 22 Ⓒ 38 Ⓓ 21

12. Which number sentence is not missing 7?

Ⓐ 13 – 6 = ☐ Ⓑ 14 – ☐ = 7

Ⓒ 15 – 7 = ☐ Ⓓ 16 – 9 = ☐

13.

$$\begin{array}{r} 821 \\ -\ 19 \\ \hline \end{array}$$

Ⓐ 819 Ⓑ 818 Ⓒ 802 Ⓓ 801

14. How many problems equal 5?

16 – 8 = ☐ 13 – 8 = ☐

12 – ☐ = 7 17 – ☐ = 8

Ⓐ 1 Ⓑ 2

Ⓒ 3 Ⓓ 4

15.

$$\begin{array}{r} 801 \\ -\ 490 \\ \hline \end{array}$$

Ⓐ 311 Ⓑ 491 Ⓒ 401 Ⓓ 411

16. How many problems are equal to nine?

18 – 9 = ☐ 17 – 8 = ☐

15 – ☐ = 6 16 – ☐ = 8

Ⓐ 1 Ⓑ 2

Ⓒ 3 Ⓓ 4

GO ON

Name

Unit 5 Test

17.

$$\begin{array}{r} 945 \\ -\ 266 \\ \hline \end{array}$$

679	779	721	627
Ⓐ	Ⓑ	Ⓒ	Ⓓ

18. Which is correct regrouping?

6 13 / ~~63~~	6 30 / ~~63~~	5 3 / ~~63~~	5 13 / ~~63~~
Ⓐ	Ⓑ	Ⓒ	Ⓓ

19.

$$\begin{array}{r} 973 \\ -\ 651 \\ \hline \end{array}$$

302	322	312	332
Ⓐ	Ⓑ	Ⓒ	Ⓓ

20. Which is the best estimate?

$$\begin{array}{r} 714 \\ -\ 232 \\ \hline \end{array}$$

300	400	500	200
Ⓐ	Ⓑ	Ⓒ	Ⓓ

Write a subtraction problem. Use 2-digit numbers that need to be regrouped. Find the answer.

STOP

Name

Counting coins up to half-dollars

Unit 6

The best way to count money is to begin with the most valuable coins and work your way down. Example:

50¢ 75¢ 85¢ 90¢ 95¢ 96¢ 97¢

Write the value of each tree on its trunk.

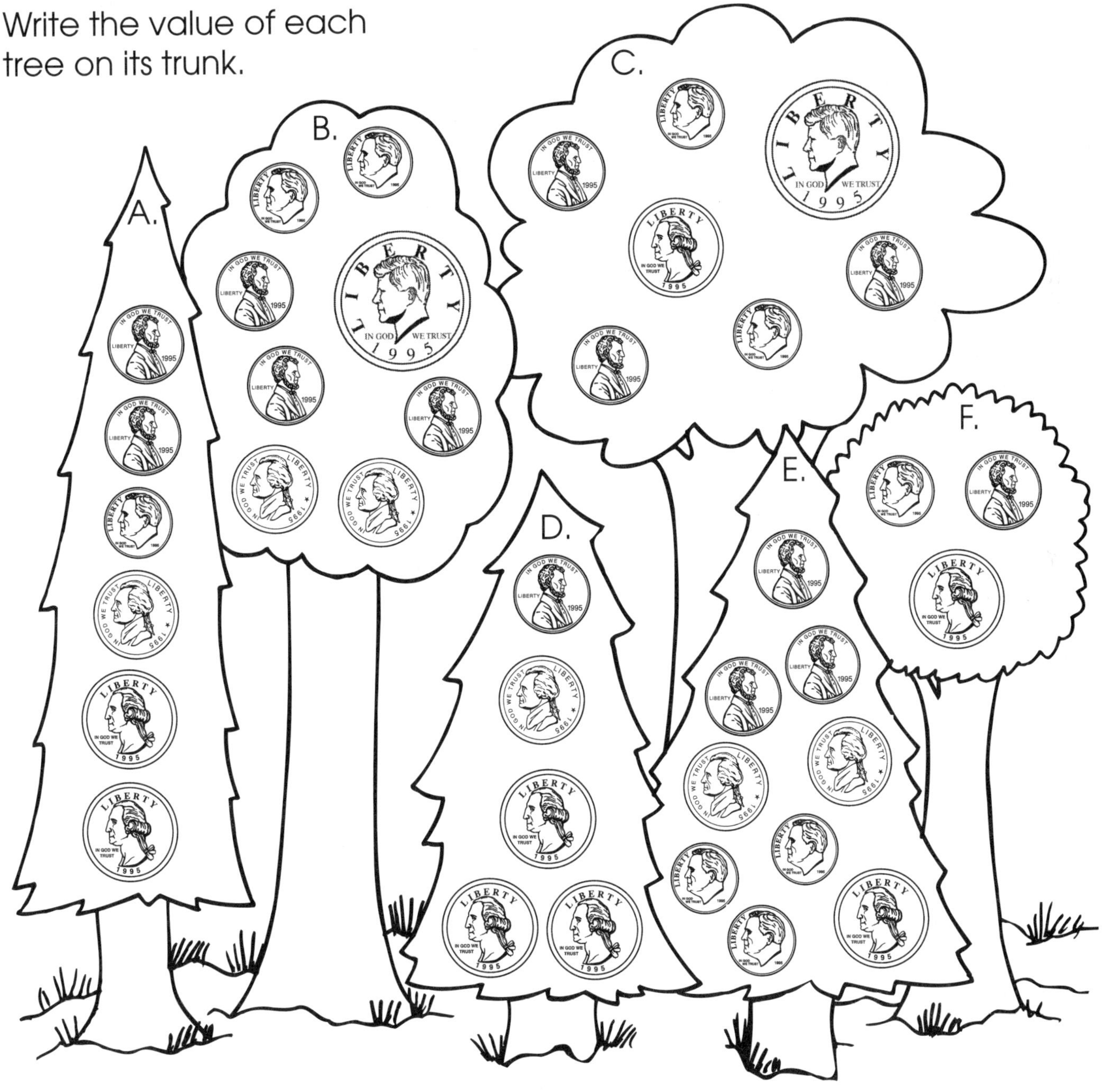

Name

Calculating change

Unit 6

When money is spent, there is often change due back to you. To find your change, make a subtraction problem. Begin with the amount of money you have, then take away the amount that is spent. Example:

		8 11
you have	→	91¢
you spend	→	− 68¢
your change	→	23¢

Use the price tags to help you write a subtraction problem and find the amount of change you will receive.

A.

you have ☐ ¢

you spend − ☐ ¢

your change = ☐ ¢

B.

you have ☐ ¢

you spend − ☐ ¢

your change = ☐ ¢

C.

you have ☐ ¢

you spend − ☐ ¢

your change = ☐ ¢

D.

you have ☐ ¢

you spend − ☐ ¢

your change = ☐ ¢

Name

Telling time to 5-minute intervals

Unit 6

The short hand on a clock tells the hour. Always use the last number that the hour hand has passed. The long hand tells the minutes. Always count by 5s when reading the long hand.

Write the times.

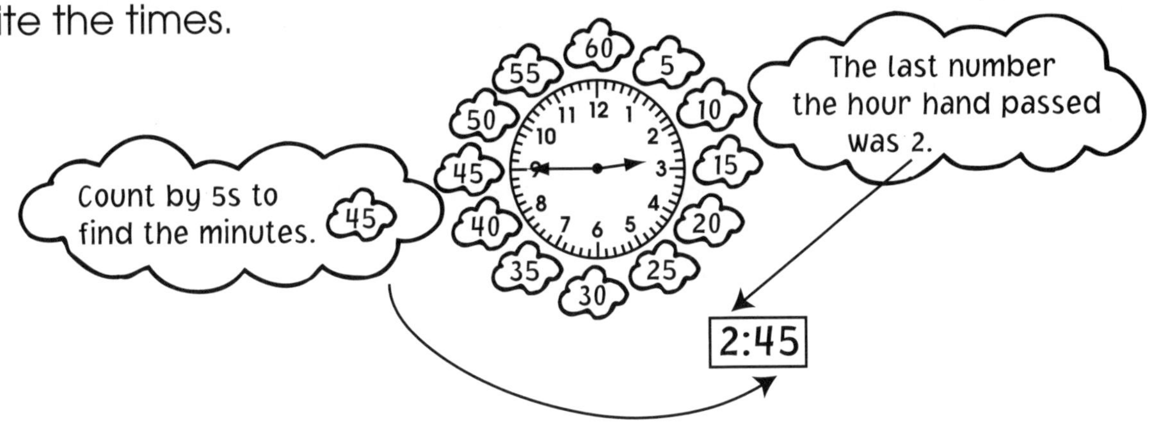

Count by 5s to find the minutes.
45
The last number the hour hand passed was 2.
2:45

A.
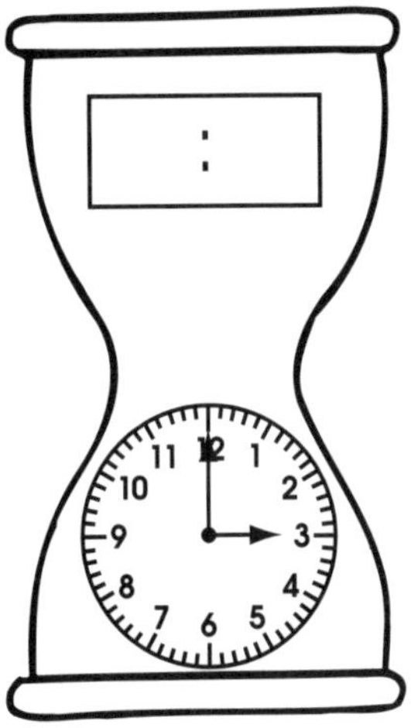

B.
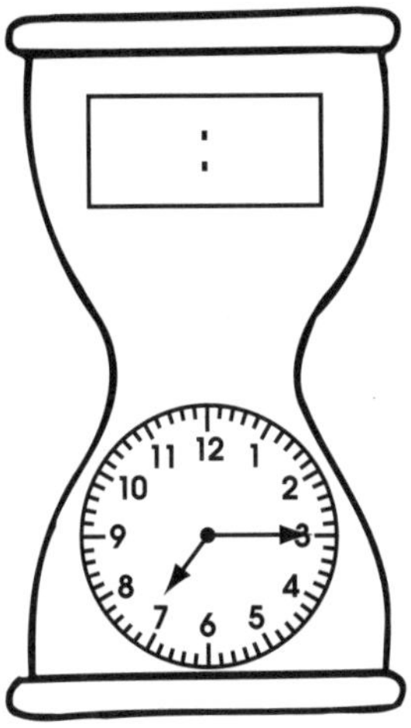

C.
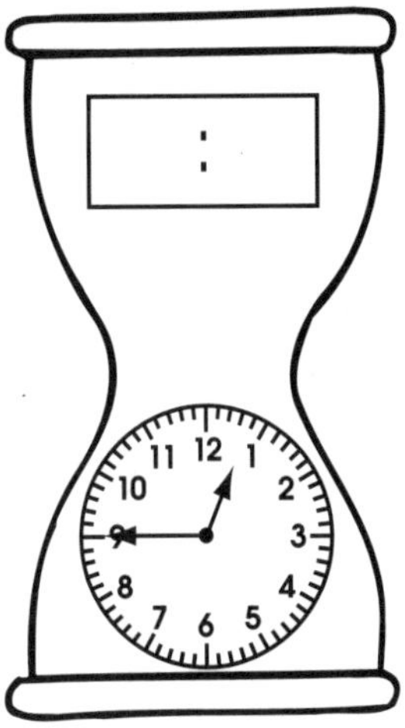

D.
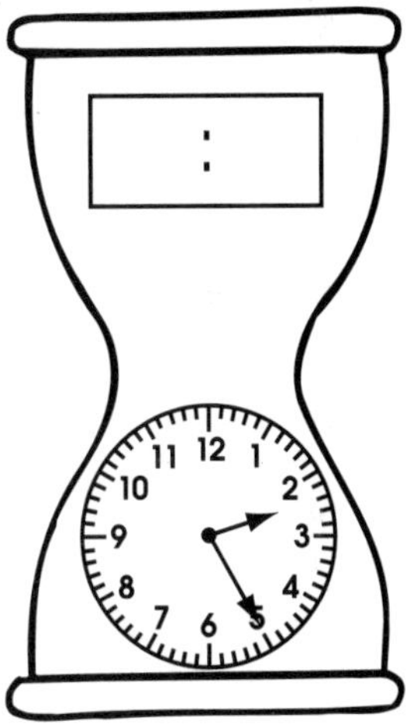

E.
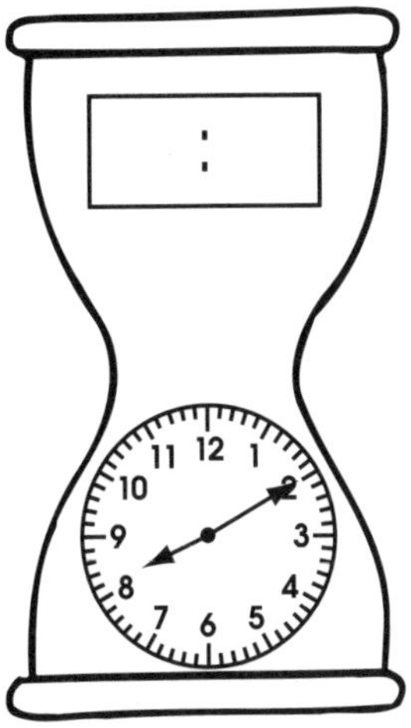

F.
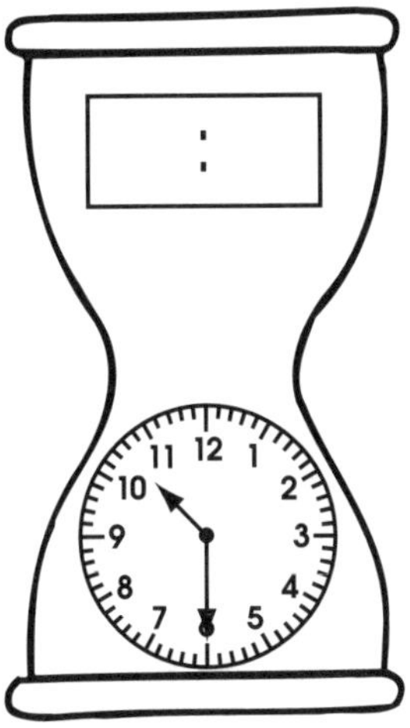

G.
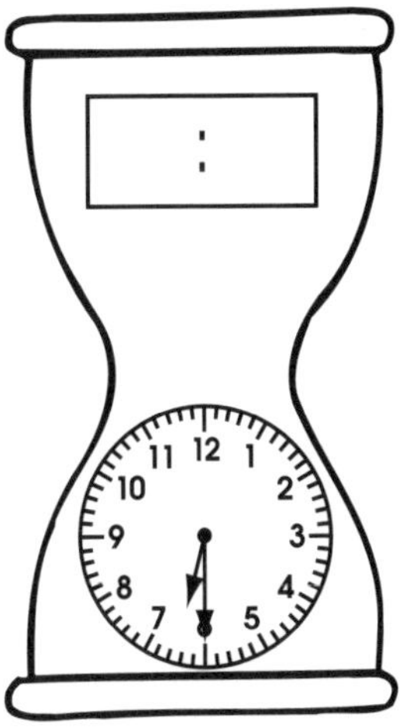

H.
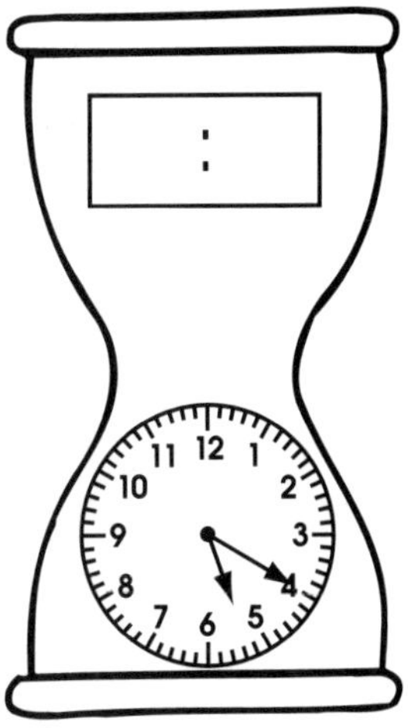

Name

Telling time using descriptors

Unit 6

Time can be named in many ways. Have you heard these phrases?

15 minutes past 1:00
quarter after 1:00

30 minutes past 1:00
half past 1:00

45 minutes past 1:00
quarter till 2:00
15 minutes before 2:00

Draw the hands on the clocks to match the times described.

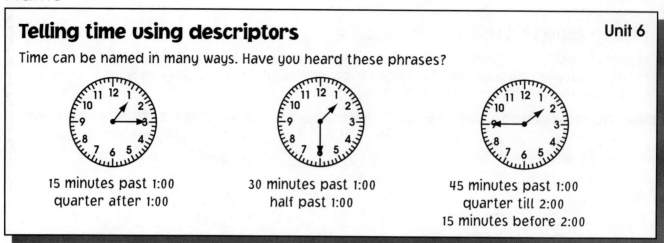

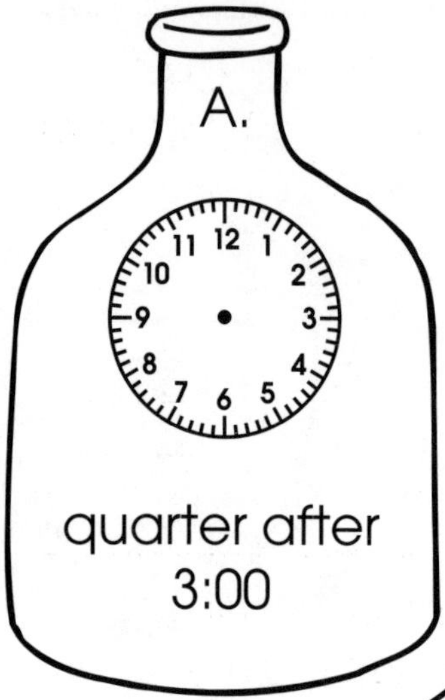

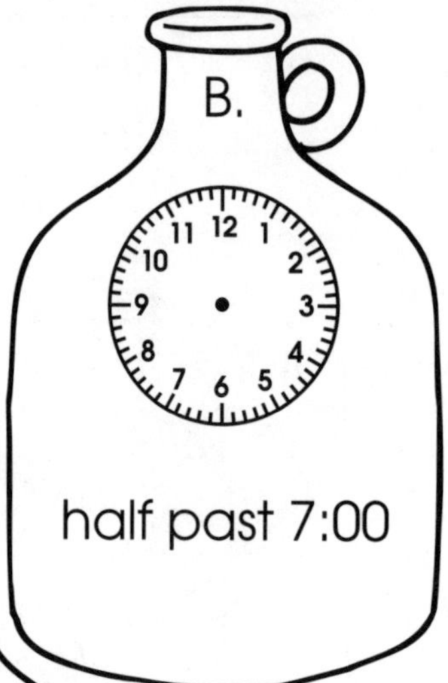

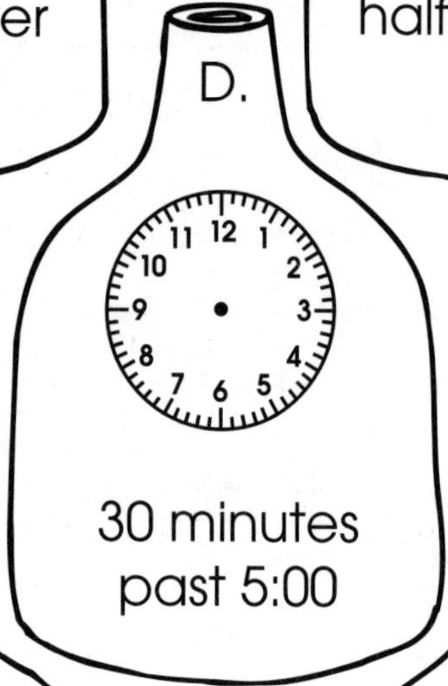

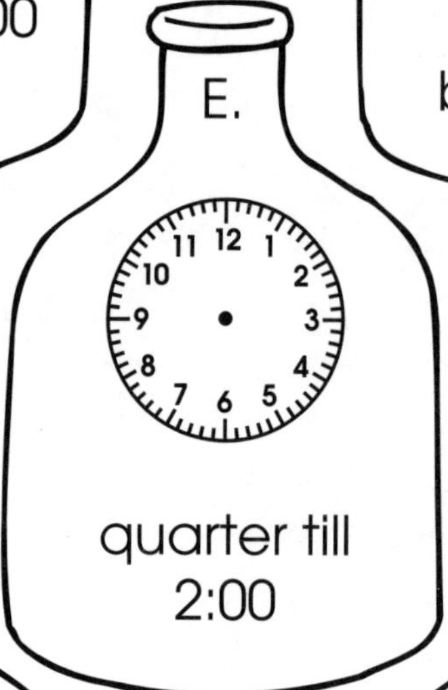

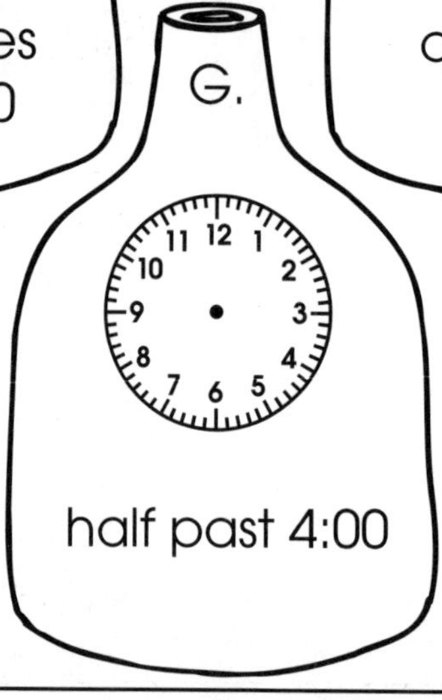

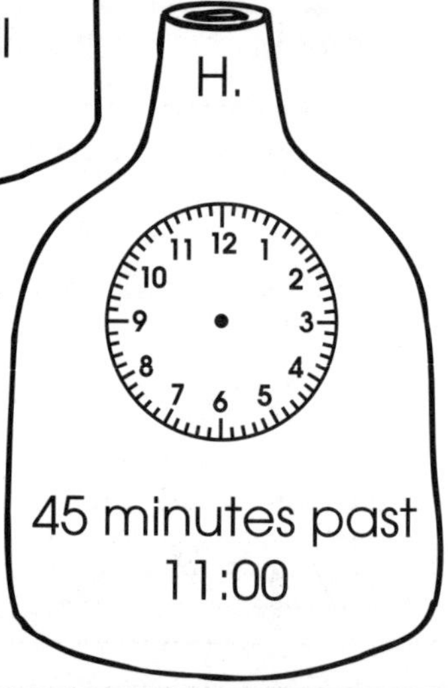

Name

Telling elapsed time

Unit 6

To find passed time, picture a clock in your mind or draw a quick one on paper. Imagine the clock showing the beginning time, then the end time. How has the clock changed? Count the minutes by fives and the hours by ones. Example:

The show started at 8:00.
It ended at 9:30.
How long did the show last?

The minute hand has moved 30.
The hour hand has moved 1.
So . . . 1 hour 30 minutes.

Start End

Use the clocks to help you find the answers.

A. The dancing dogs came on at 6:15. They danced until 6:45. How long did they dance?

____

B. The clowns started at 7:00. They rode bikes for 40 minutes. What time did they end?

____

C. The lion tamer started at 4:00. He was on stage until 5:30. How long did he perform?

____

D. The elephants came on at 5:20. They performed for 1 hour. What time did they finish?

____

E. The tightrope walker began at 8:40. She finished at 9:05. How long was she walking?

____

F. The human rocket came on at 9:45. He shot off the stage 10 minutes later. What time did he leave?

____

Name

Interpreting a calendar

Unit 6

Reading a calendar is like reading a book. The days of the week go from left to right, like sentences. The weeks go from top to bottom, like paragraphs. Be careful, some calendars split a square to make room for the last days of the month. Look at the last Sunday of this month!

Use the calendar to find the answers.

June

Sunday	Monday	Tuesday	Wednesday	Thursday	Friday	Saturday
						1
2	3	4	5	6	7	8
9	10	11	12	13	14	15
16	17	18	19	20	21	22
23 / 30	24	25	26	27	28	29

A. How many Wednesdays are in the month? ________

B. What day of the week is the 30th? ________________

C. How many days are in the month? ________

D. What is the date of the third Friday? ________

E. What is the date of the first Monday? ________

F. How many Sundays are in the month? ________

Find your birthday month on a calendar. Write three questions about the month.

Name

Choosing and estimating units of measurement

Unit 6

This chart shows the different ways to measure. The standard units are listed first.
The metric units are listed second.

 pounds kilograms	 inches centimeters	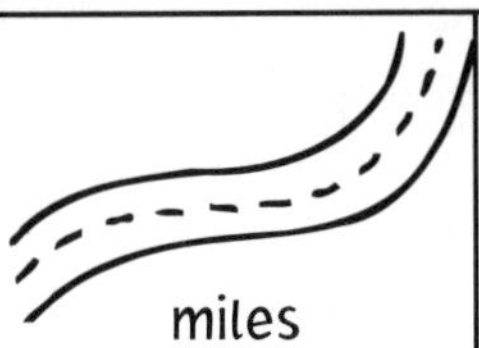 miles kilometers	 °F °C	 gallons liters

Use the chart to help you choose the best estimate.

A.

50 pounds   5 pounds   5 gallons

B.

3 pounds   3 gallons   3 kilometers

C.

80° F   80 gallons   8° F

D.

10 miles   10 gallons   10 inches

E.

18 inches   18 pounds   18° F

F.

80° F   8 cm   30° F

G.

2 liters   2 pounds   2 miles

H.

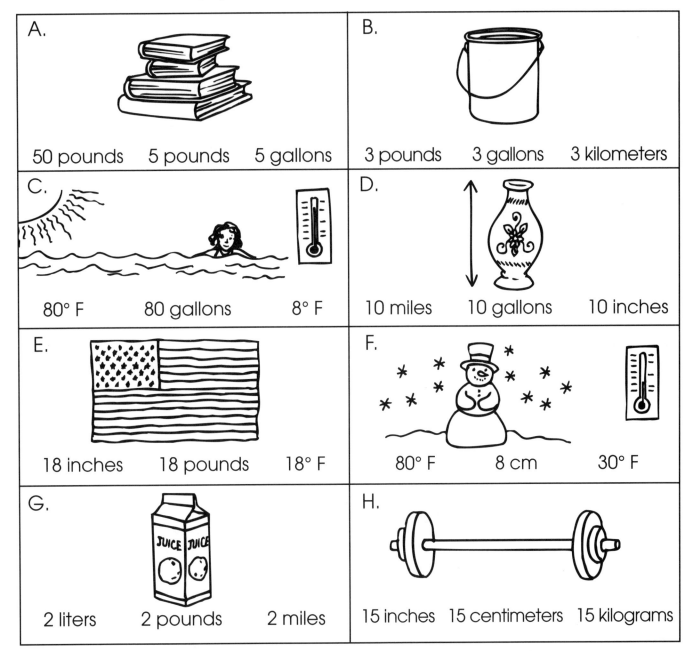

15 inches   15 centimeters   15 kilograms

Name

Measuring length using inches and centimeters

Unit 6

Have you ever noticed that some rulers have numbers on both sides? One side shows inches and the other shows centimeters. To measure length, place the starting point of your ruler on the beginning of the line. Then read the nearest number at the end of the line.

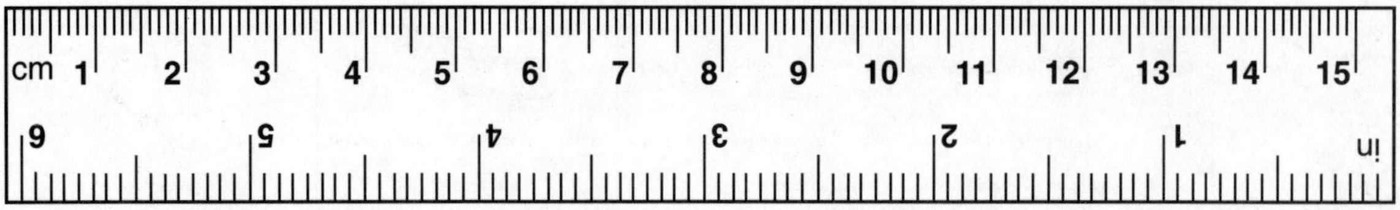

Iggy the Lizard and Slinky the Salamander are feasting in the garden. Measure their paths on page 89. Use the inch side of your ruler for Iggy. Iggy's path is the solid line. Use the centimeter side for Slinky. Slinky's path is the broken line.

—— Iggy's Inches ——

Start at 

On to  ☐ in.

On to  ☐ in.

On to  ☐ in.

Last to  ☐ in.

Total ☐ in.

- - - Slinky's Centimeters - - -

Start at 

On to  ☐ cm

On to  ☐ cm

On to  ☐ cm

Last to  ☐ cm

Total ☐ cm

Name

Measuring length

Unit 6

The Garden Map

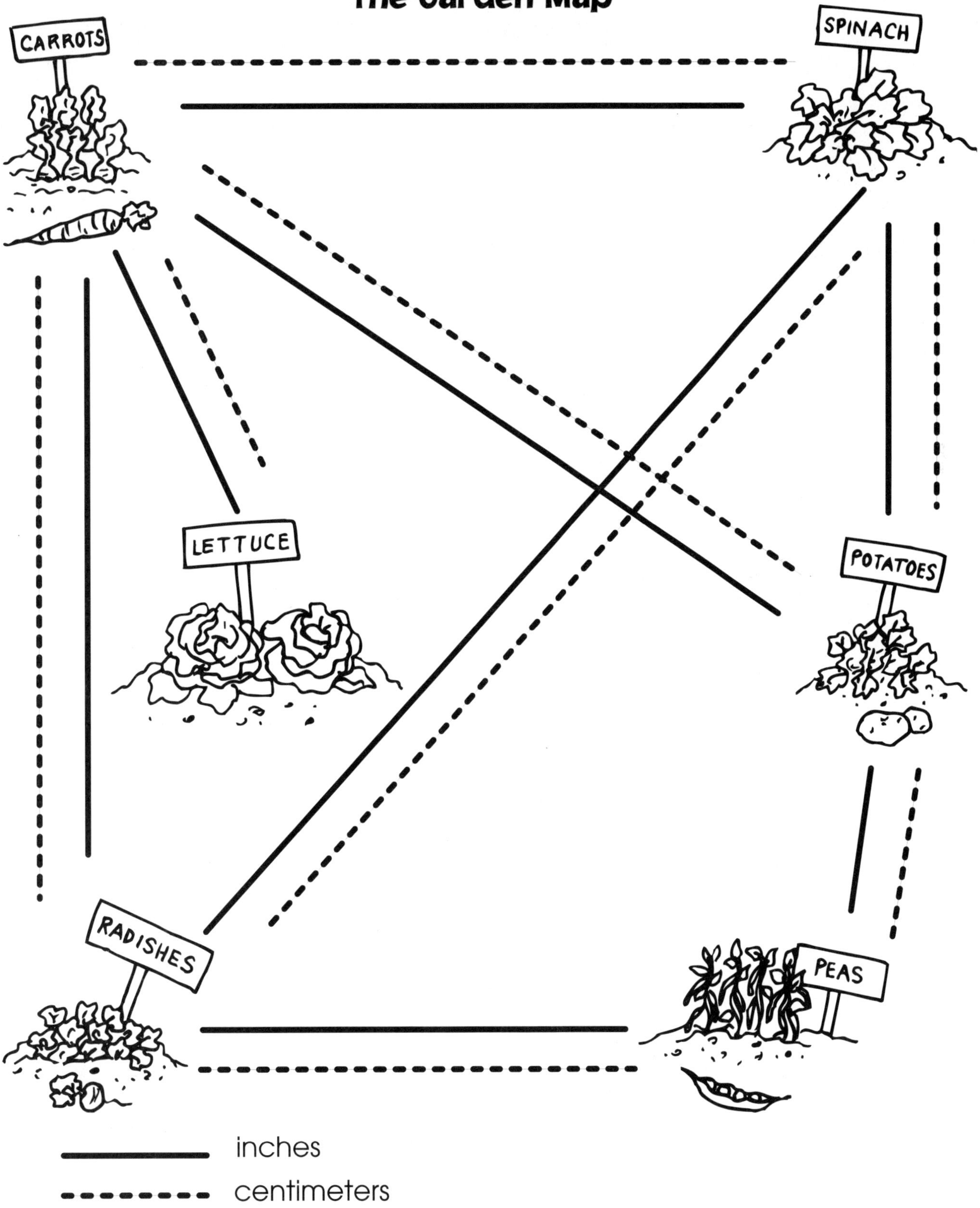

Name

Unit 6 Test

Page 1

Measurement

Read or listen to the question. Fill in the circle beside the best answer.

Use your time wisely. If a problem seems tough, skip it and come back to it later.

❑ Example:
How much money is shown?

Ⓐ 86¢ Ⓑ 91¢

Ⓒ 96¢ Ⓓ 81¢

Answer: B because 50¢ + 25¢ + 10¢ + 5¢ + 1¢ = 91¢.

Now try these. You have 20 minutes. Continue until you see STOP.

1. What time is shown?

3:45	2:45	9:15	9:10
Ⓐ	Ⓑ	Ⓒ	Ⓓ

2. Which measurements are correct for the length of the line?

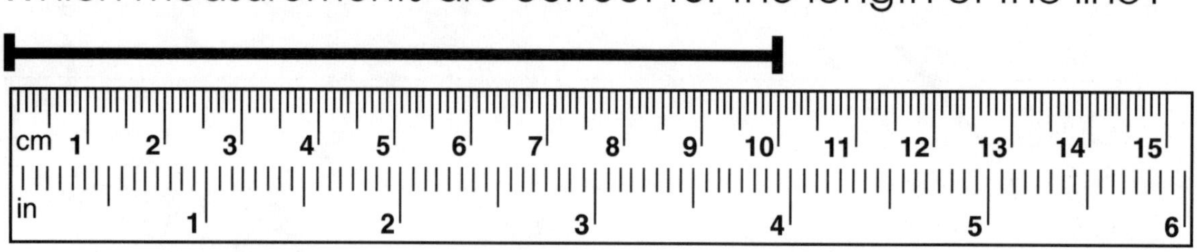

Ⓐ 4 in. 10 cm

Ⓑ 4 in. 4 cm

Ⓒ 2 in. 10 cm

Ⓓ 10 in. 4 cm

GO ON

Name

Unit 6 Test

Page 2

3. You have:  You find a nickel.

How much do you have now?

Ⓐ	Ⓑ	Ⓒ	Ⓓ
61¢	66¢	76¢	71¢

4. Which group of coins does not equal 20¢?

 Ⓐ

 Ⓑ

 Ⓒ

 Ⓓ

5. How much change will you get if you pay with 2 quarters?

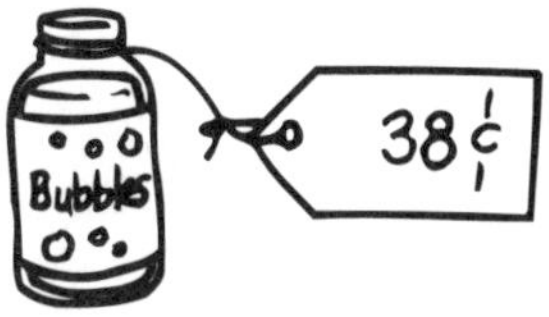

Ⓐ	Ⓑ	Ⓒ	Ⓓ
22¢	12¢	32¢	28¢

6. Which clock shows 9:25?

 Ⓐ

 Ⓑ

 Ⓒ

 Ⓓ

7. How long did the concert last?

Concert Started

Concert Ended

Ⓐ 1 hour

Ⓑ 1 hour 30 minutes

Ⓒ 2 hours

Ⓓ 2 hours 30 minutes

GO ON

Name

Unit 6 Test

Page 3

8. Count the coins.

(A) 95¢ (B) 80¢

(C) 90¢ (D) 85¢

9. How many pencils are more than 8 cm long?

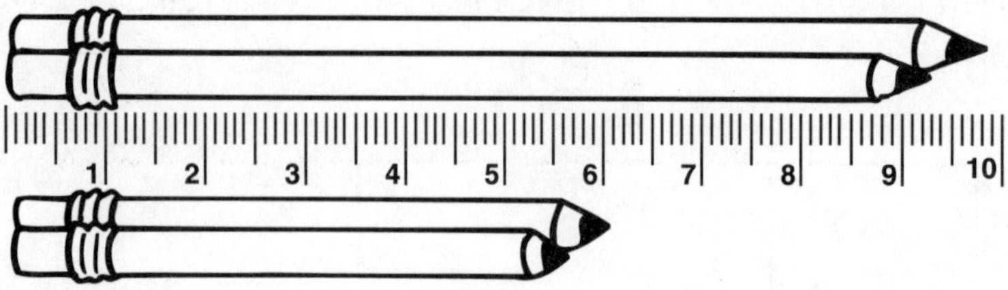

(A) 1 (B) 2

(C) 3 (D) 4

10. Which clock shows half past noon?

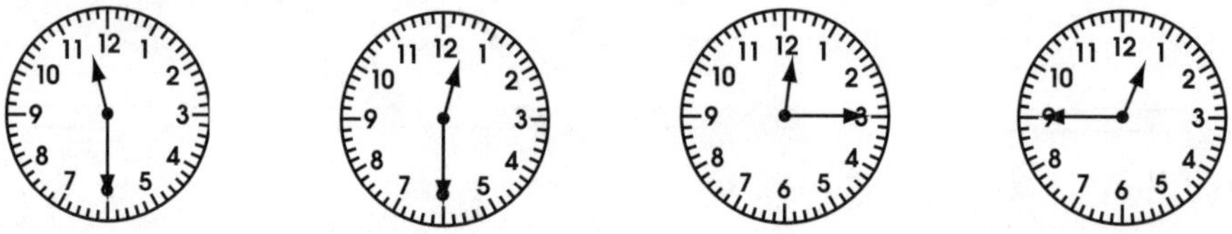

(A) (B) (C) (D)

Use the calendar below for questions 11–13.

March

Sun.	Mon.	Tues.	Wed.	Thurs.	Fri.	Sat.
				1	2	3
4	5	6	7	8	9	10
11	12	13	14	15	16	17
18	19	20	21	22	23	24
25	26	27	28	29	30	31

11. How many Thursdays are in March?

one (A) eight (B) four (C) five (D)

GO ON

Name

Unit 6 Test

12. Which date is not a Wednesday?

March 26 (A)   March 7 (B)   March 28 (C)   March 14 (D)

13. What is the date on the 3rd Monday in March?

March 5 (A)   March 19 (B)   March 3 (C)   March 26 (D)

14. Which unit measures temperature?

gallon (A)   inches (B)   °F (C)   pounds (D)

15. Which real-life object would be about five inches tall?

(A)

(B)

(C)

(D)

16. Which time shows quarter after 2:00?

(A)

(B)

(C)

(D)

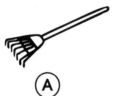

17. The school play started at 7:00. It lasted 1 hour and 30 minutes. What time did the play end?

7:30 (A)   8:30 (B)   8:00 (C)   9:30 (D)

GO ON

Name

Unit 6 Test

Page 5

18. How tall is the can?

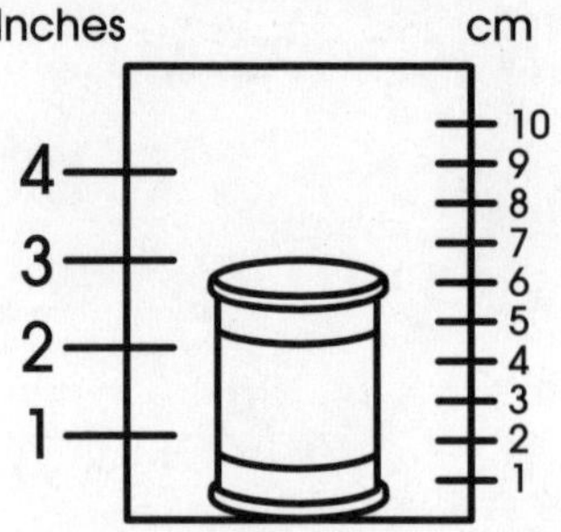

Ⓐ 6 cm
Ⓑ 2 in.
Ⓒ 3 in.
Ⓓ 9 cm

19. Sam spends 72¢. He pays with these coins. How much change will he get?

Ⓐ 5¢
Ⓑ 2¢
Ⓒ 13¢
Ⓓ 3¢

20. Which real-life object weighs about 10 pounds?

Ⓐ Ⓑ Ⓒ Ⓓ

This piggy bank has 29¢ in savings. Draw the coins.

STOP

Name

Probability **Unit 7**

Mrs. Nickles gives her class a piece of candy at the end of each day. As one of her students, you can predict which piece of candy you are most likely to get by finding which type of candy is in the jar the most. Example:

You have the best chance of choosing a  . You are least likely to choose a  .

Use the pictures to predict the outcomes for each day.

A. Which candy is most likely to be chosen on:

Monday ____________

Tuesday ____________

Wednesday ____________

Thursday ____________

Friday ____________

B. Which candy is least likely to be chosen on:

Monday ____________

Tuesday ____________

Wednesday ____________

Thursday ____________

Friday ____________

Monday

Thursday

Tuesday

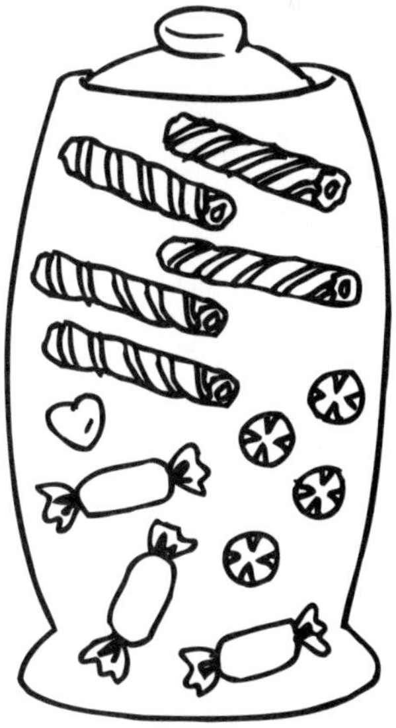

Friday

Wednesday

Name

Interpreting a bar graph

Unit 7

A **bar graph** makes it easy to compare information. (This bar graph will show the total number of candies that Mrs. Nickles gave away on page 95.)

Use the jars on page 95 to complete the bar graph. Starting at the bottom, color a square for every candy that Mrs. Nickles passed out. The finished graph will help you answer the questions.

Candy Mrs. Nickles Passed Out

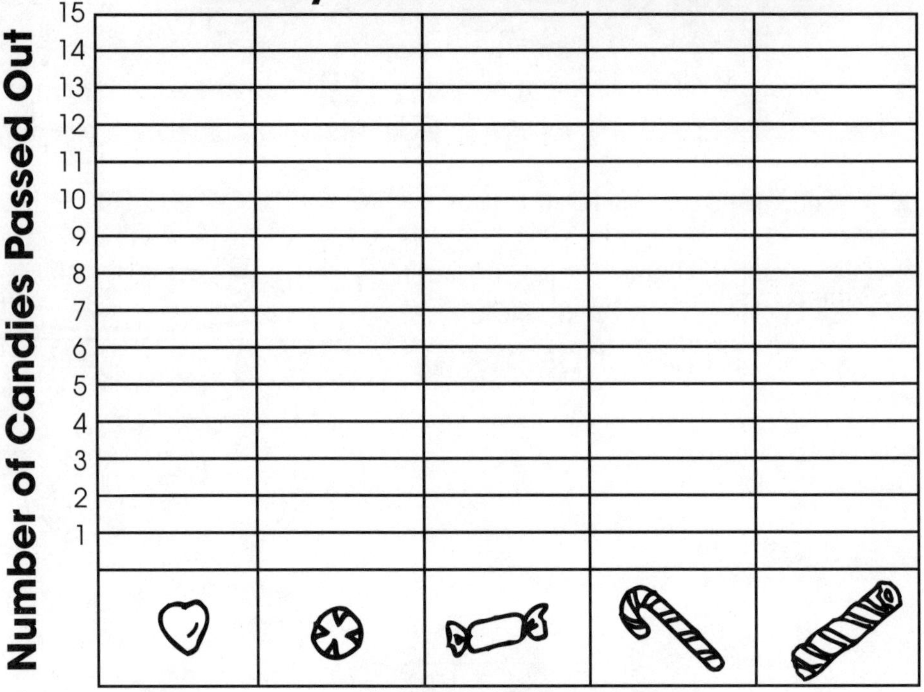

Types of Candy

A. Which candy totaled 11 pieces? ______________

B. Which two candies combined total 23 pieces?
______________ and ______________

C. How many more pieces of  than  are there? _________

D. How many pieces of  and  together did Mrs. Nickles give away? _________

E. Which two candies combined total 21 pieces?
______________ and ______________

F. How many more pieces of  than  are there? _________

G. What is the total number of pieces of , , and ?
____

Name

Interpreting a tally chart **Unit 7**

Tally marks look like this: III. They are used to keep the count of something.
To make it easier to count the tally marks, they are grouped in fives like this: 卌.

	⚀	⚁	⚂	⚃	⚄	⚅
King	卌 III	卌 卌 II	卌	卌 卌 I	卌 IIII	卌 II
Queen	卌 I	卌 卌 卌 III	卌 卌	卌 III	卌 卌 II	III
Prince	III	卌	卌 卌 卌	卌	卌 II	卌
Princess	卌 卌	卌 卌 卌 II	卌	卌 IIII	卌 卌	卌 I

The Royal family is playing a game using one die. Their rolls are tallied on the chart. Use the information to answer the questions.

A. How many threes did the prince roll? ________

B. How many sixes were rolled in all? ________

C. Who rolled a total of 17 twos? ________________

D. How many fours did the king and the queen roll altogether? ________

E. Who rolled a total of 12 fives? ________________

F. How many more ones did the princess roll than the queen? ________

G. How many threes were rolled in all? ________

H. Who rolled the fewest fours? ________________

Name

Interpreting data from a table

Unit 7

Information can be gathered from a **table** like the one below.

This table shows the number of men in the two kings' courts. Use the data to answer the questions.

	Knights	Dukes	Guards	Counts	Jesters
King Ludwig	11	9	42	16	19
King Johans	8	9	29	13	27

A. How many knights and dukes does King Johans have? ________

B. How many more guards does King Ludwig have than King Johans? ________

C. Who has 16 counts? ________________________

D. How many guards and jesters does King Ludwig have? ________

E. Who has 38 dukes and guards combined? ______________________

F. Which king has more counts and jesters combined? ______________

G. Who has the fewest knights? ________________________

Name

Interpreting a grid

Unit 7

A **grid** shows the location of something. It has lines that are numbered and/or lettered. To describe the location of the  on this grid, you write (B, 4) because the tulips are found at the intersection of lines B and 4.

Write the location of each of the plants.

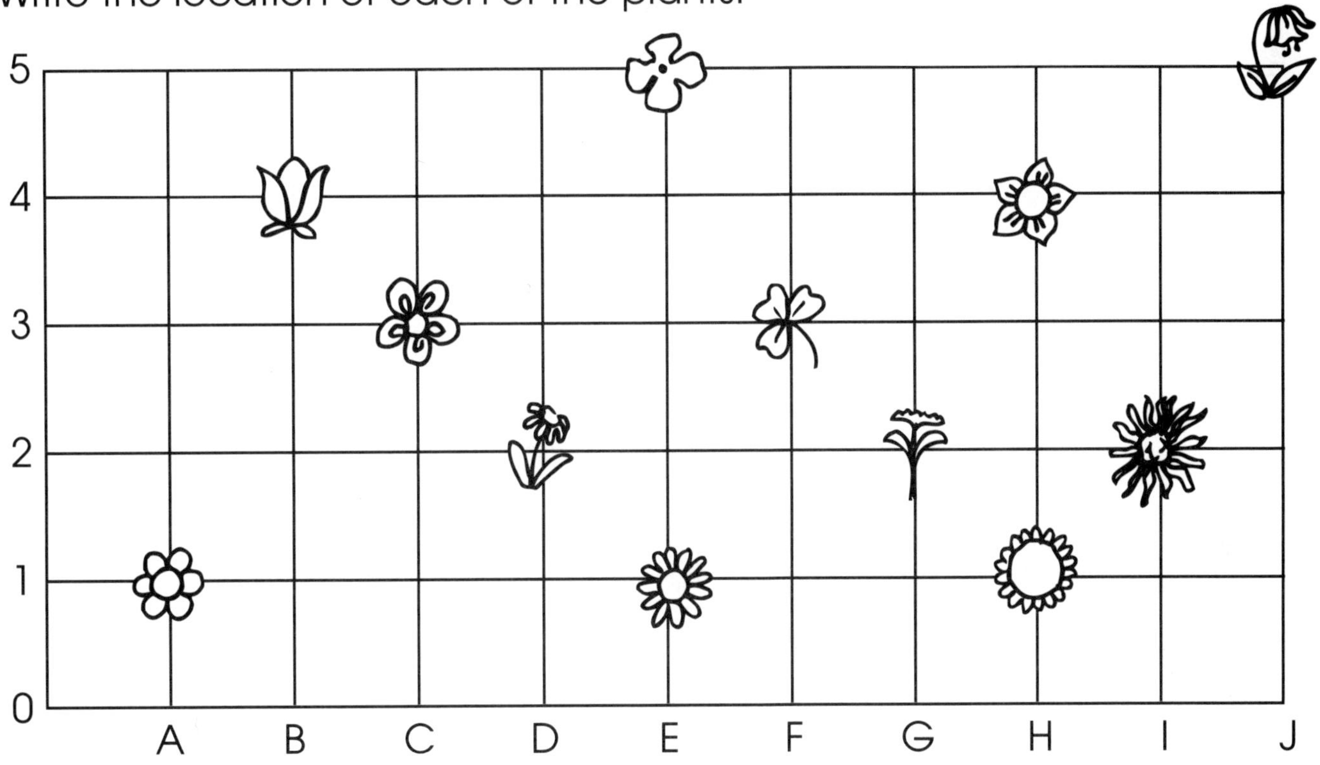

Draw the plant found at each location.

A. (D, 2) =

B. (E, 5) =

C. (H, 4) =

D. (H, 1) =

E. (I, 2) =

F. (C, 3) =

G. (F, 3) =

H. (E, 1) =

I. (J, 5) =

J. (A, 1) =

K. (G, 2) =

L. (B, 4) =

Name

Interpreting a picture graph

Unit 7

A **picture graph** is another way to record information. Picture graphs often have a key that will tell what each picture means. In this graph, 1 seed picture represents 2 seeds.

Use the picture graph to find the answers.

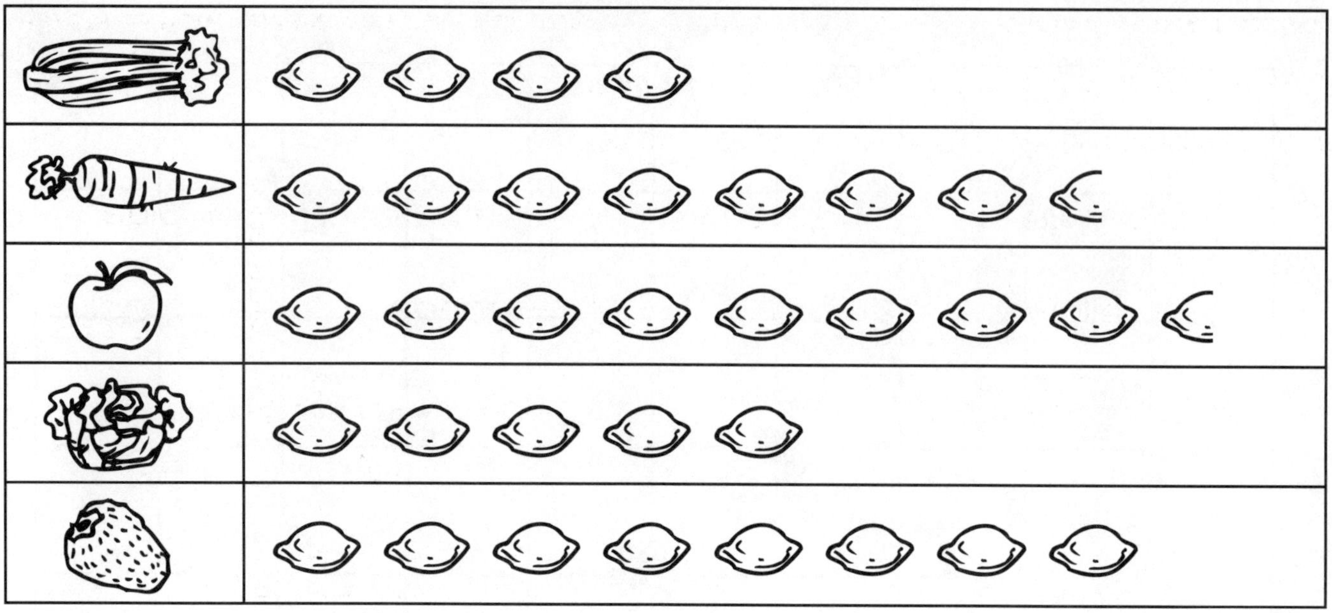

 = 2 seeds

A. How many celery seeds are there? ________

B. How many carrot seeds are there? ________

C. Which plant has 17 seeds? ____________________

D. How many more apple seeds are there than lettuce seeds?

____

E. How many strawberry and apple seeds are there? ________

F. Which plant has the fewest seeds? ____________________

G. How many more carrot seeds than celery seeds are there? ________

H. How many apple and carrot seeds are there in all? ________

Name

Identifying fractions as part of a group

Unit 7

Fractions describe part of a group. Example:

number of stars → 5
total number of shapes in group → 8

$$\frac{5}{8}$$

Compare the number of stars to the total number of shapes on each football. Color the footballs using the code.

$\frac{1}{2}$ = brown	$\frac{2}{3}$ = green	$\frac{3}{4}$ = purple	$\frac{3}{8}$ = blue
$\frac{1}{3}$ = yellow	$\frac{1}{4}$ = red	$\frac{1}{8}$ = orange	$\frac{5}{8}$ = black

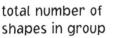

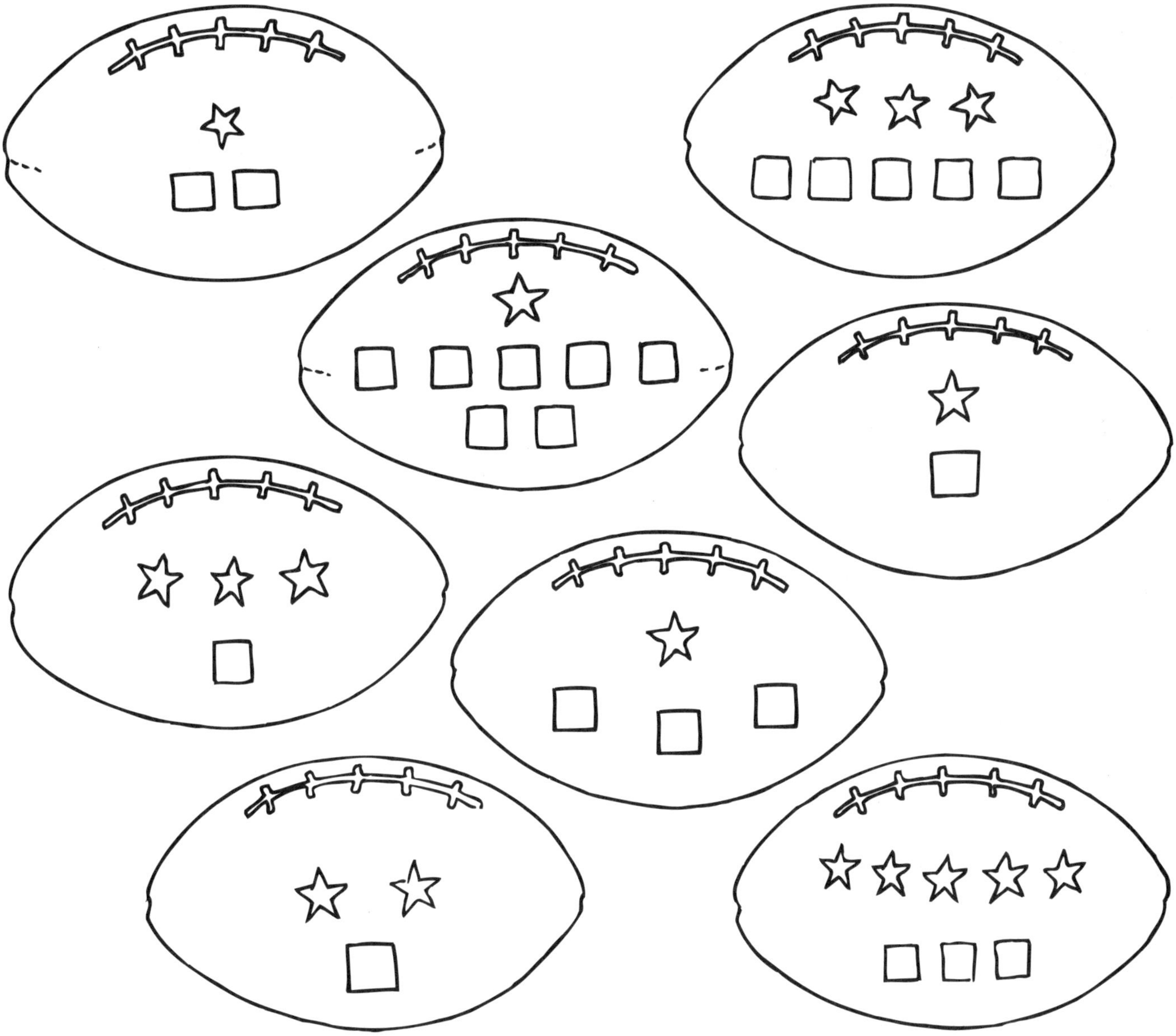

Name

Identifying fractions as part of a whole

Unit 7

This circle has been divided into equal parts, so it can also be described as a fraction.
Examples:

(shaded square) = $\frac{3}{4}$ ← (shaded square) parts; ← total parts

(unshaded square) = $\frac{1}{4}$ ← (unshaded square) parts; ← total parts

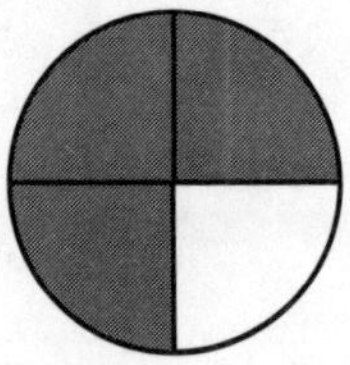

Color the circles as directed.

A.

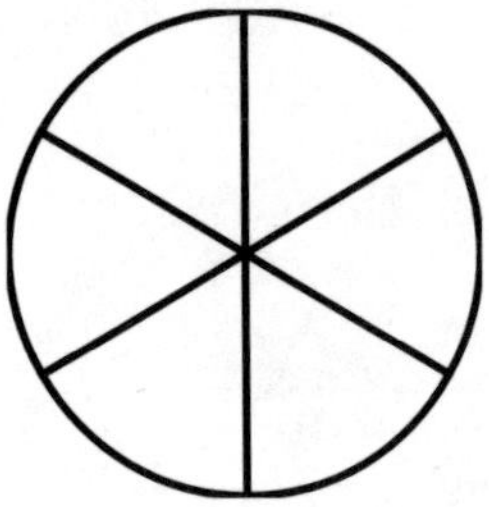

$\frac{1}{6}$ = red

$\frac{2}{6}$ = yellow

$\frac{3}{6}$ = blue

B.

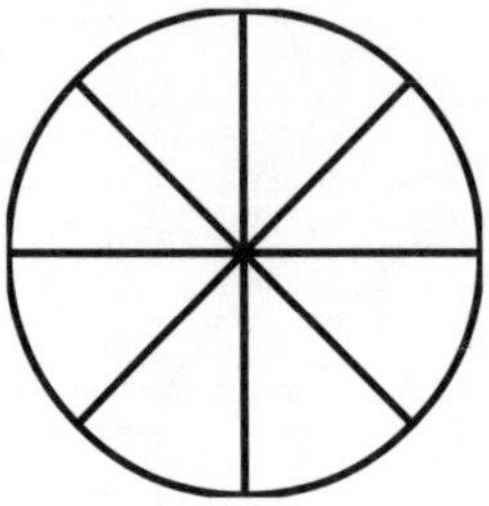

$\frac{3}{8}$ = purple

$\frac{2}{8}$ = brown

$\frac{3}{8}$ = red

C.

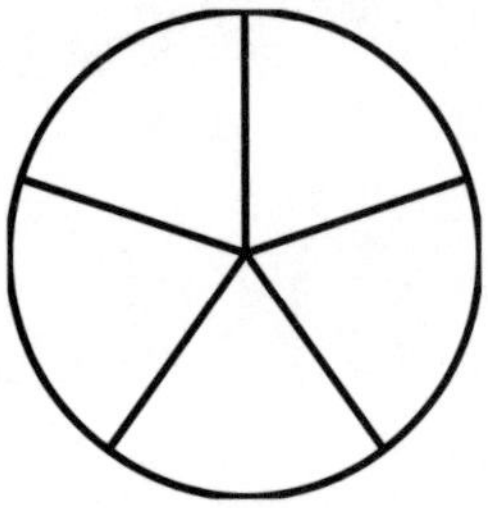

$\frac{1}{5}$ = red

$\frac{2}{5}$ = blue

$\frac{2}{5}$ = purple

D.

$\frac{1}{3}$ = yellow

$\frac{2}{3}$ = orange

E.

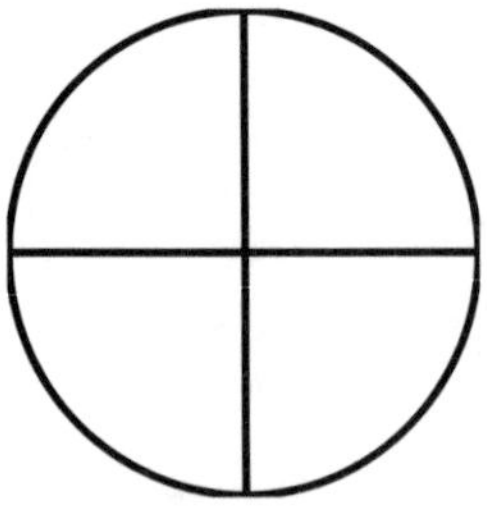

$\frac{1}{4}$ = blue

$\frac{3}{4}$ = purple

F.

$\frac{2}{7}$ = red

$\frac{1}{7}$ = orange

$\frac{4}{7}$ = blue

Name

Unit 7 Test

Statistics, Fractions

Read or listen to the question. Fill in the circle beside the best answer.

❑ Example:
Which group shows $\frac{3}{4}$ of the group as rectangles?

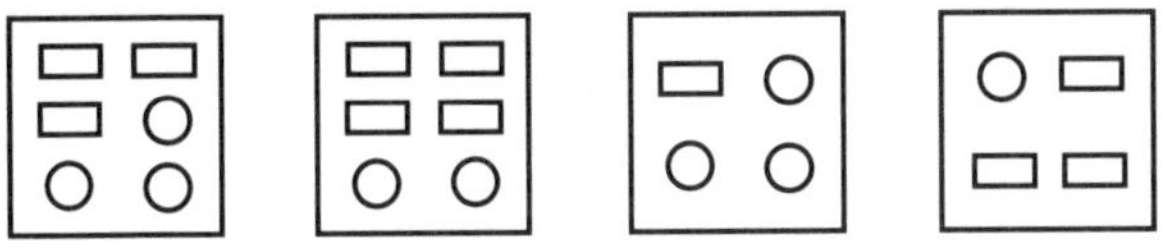

Ⓐ Ⓑ Ⓒ Ⓓ

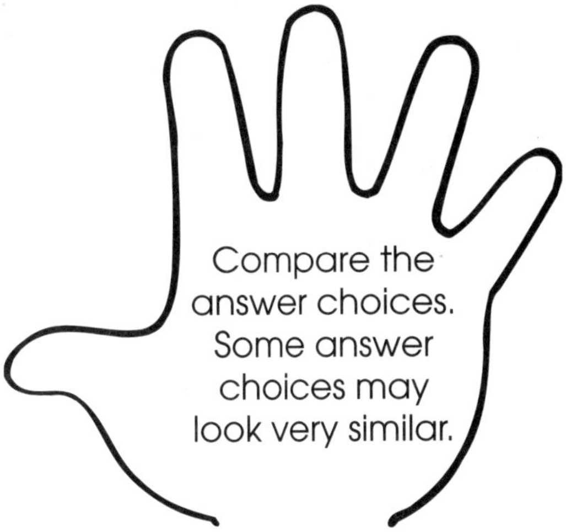

Compare the answer choices. Some answer choices may look very similar.

Answer: D because there are 4 total shapes and 3 of them are rectangles.

Now try these. You have 20 minutes. Continue until you see STOP.

1. Which is most likely to be chosen?

Ⓐ Ⓑ Ⓒ Ⓓ

2. Which will probably not be chosen?

Ⓐ Ⓑ Ⓒ Ⓓ

3. What part of the group is spotted?

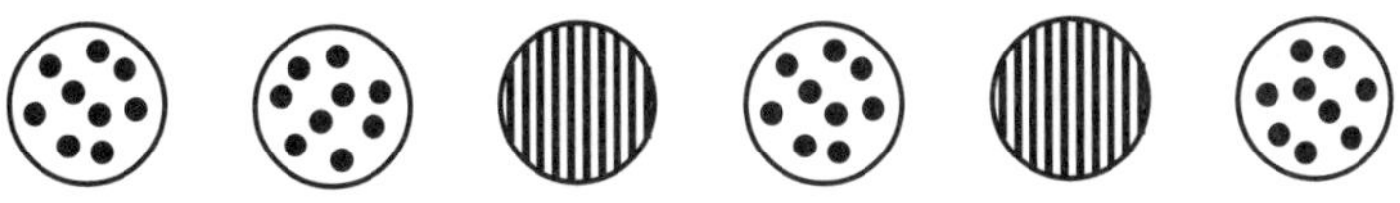

Ⓐ $\frac{2}{6}$ Ⓑ $\frac{6}{2}$

Ⓒ $\frac{4}{6}$ Ⓓ $\frac{6}{4}$

4. Which picture shows $\frac{2}{3}$ shaded?

Ⓐ Ⓑ Ⓒ Ⓓ

GO ON

Name

Unit 7 Test

Page 2

Use the bar graph to the right for 5–7.

Fish Caught

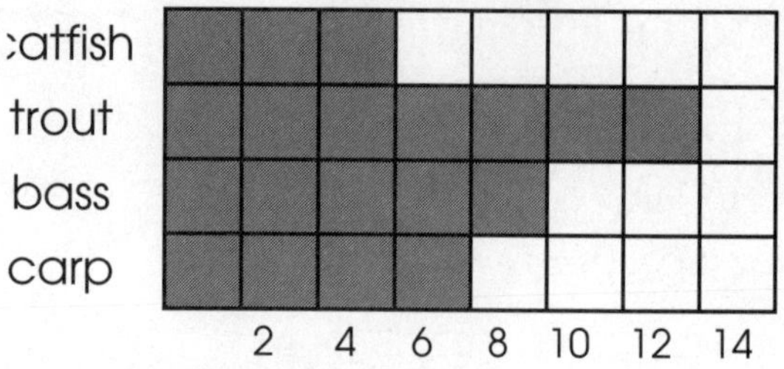

5. How many bass and catfish were caught?

16 Ⓐ 18 Ⓑ 14 Ⓒ 6 Ⓓ

6. How many more trout than carp were caught?

4 Ⓐ 3 Ⓑ 5 Ⓒ 6 Ⓓ

7. Which type of fish was caught the least?

catfish Ⓐ trout Ⓑ bass Ⓒ carp Ⓓ

Use the tally chart to the right for 8–10.

Books We Have Read

	paperbacks	hardbacks	books with tapes
Matthew	|||	𝍸 |	𝍸 |||
Anna	𝍸	||	𝍸 |
Laura	||||	𝍸 ||	𝍸 |||

8. How many paperbacks were read in all?

12 Ⓐ 22 Ⓑ 15 Ⓒ 13 Ⓓ

9. Who read the most hardback books?

Matthew Ⓐ Anna Ⓑ Laura Ⓒ Anna and Matthew Ⓓ

10. Matthew and Laura read the same number of:

paperbacks Ⓐ hardbacks Ⓑ books with tapes Ⓒ nothing Ⓓ

GO ON

Name

Unit 7 Test

Use the table to the right for 11–13.

Butterfly Watch

	Mon.	Tues.	Wed.	Thurs.	Fri.
Monarchs	11	10	12	13	9
Blue Morphos	15	8	11	15	12

11. How many butterflies were spotted on Friday?

Ⓐ 21 Ⓑ 12 Ⓒ 28 Ⓓ 23

12. Which days were more monarchs spotted?

Ⓐ Mon., Tues. Ⓑ Wed., Thurs. Ⓒ Thurs., Fri. Ⓓ Tues., Wed.

13. On which two days were the same number of blue morphos spotted?

Ⓐ Mon., Wed. Ⓑ Mon., Thurs. Ⓒ Tues., Fri. Ⓓ Wed., Thurs.

Use the grid to the right for 14–16.

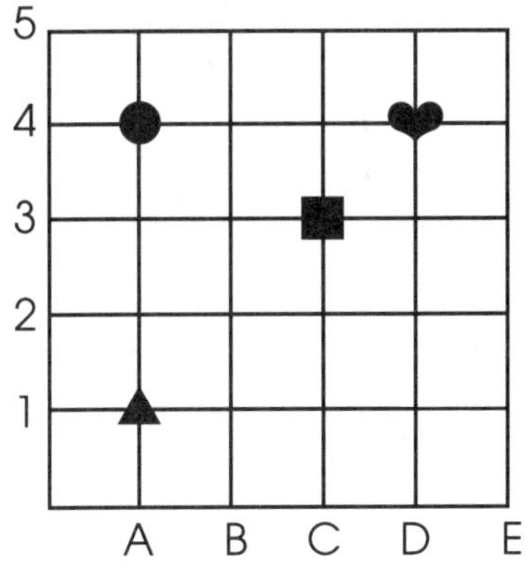

14. What shape is found at (C, 3)?

Ⓐ ▲ Ⓑ ❤ Ⓒ ● Ⓓ ■

15. Where is the ❤ located?

Ⓐ (A, 4) Ⓑ (D, 4) Ⓒ (C, 3) Ⓓ (A, 1)

16. Which two shapes are found on the line labeled A?

Ⓐ ● and ❤ Ⓑ ▲ and ■ Ⓒ ● and ▲ Ⓓ ■ and ▲

GO ON

Name

Unit 7 Test

Page 4

Use the picture graph below for 17–20.

Full Recycling Bins

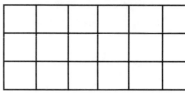

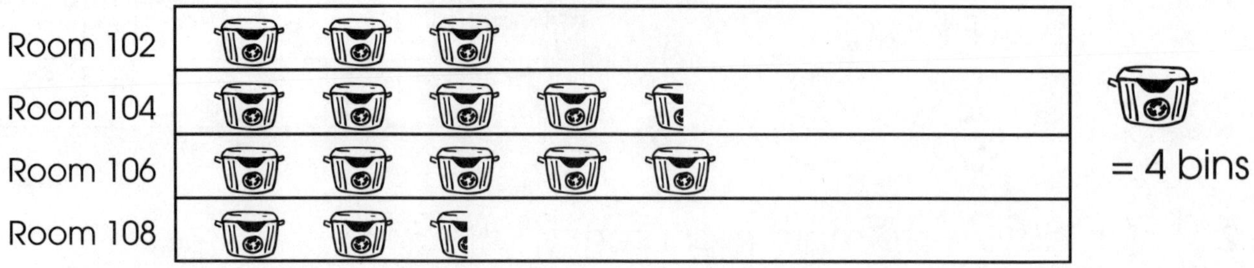

17. How many bins did Rooms 102 and 106 fill together?

(A)	(B)	(C)	(D)
20	18	24	32

18. How many bins did Room 108 fill?

(A)	(B)	(C)	(D)
8	10	12	16

19. Which room filled 18 bins?

(A)	(B)	(C)	(D)
Room 102	Room 104	Room 106	Room 108

20. How many more bins did Room 106 fill than Room 104?

(A)	(B)	(C)	(D)
2	4	6	8

Complete the bar graph to show the following:

A party of children were choosing balloons. Four of them chose blue. More chose green than blue and less chose purple than blue.

Colors of Balloons

blue						
green						
purple						

STOP

Name

Identifying key addition words

Unit 8

The problems you see on this page tell a story. Your job is to use information from the story to make a math problem and solve the problem. This is called **problem solving**. One difficult part of this is deciding whether to add or subtract. Sometimes key words in the story will help you decide. Watch for these key words that tell you to add: *altogether, total, in all, combined.* After you solve the problem, label the answer with the story unit (words to tell what the story is about).

Circle the key words in each story. Then write an addition problem and find the answer. Label the answer with the story unit.

The school play will have 14 tigers, 6 jaguars, and 16 lions. How many wild cats are there in all?

$$\begin{array}{r} {}^{1}\\ 14 \\ 6 \\ +\ 16 \\ \hline 36 \end{array}$$ wild cats

A. There are 22 boys and 27 girls in the play. How many total children are in the play?

B. Three dads and 16 moms are helping make the costumes. How many parents are there altogether?

C. The school sold 132 adult tickets and 68 children tickets. How many tickets did they sell combined?

D. There will be two shows on Friday, two shows on Saturday, and one show on Sunday. How many shows will there be in all?

E. The actors will need 14 hats, 24 coats, and 31 scarves. How many props is that combined?

Write an addition story problem. Solve the problem.

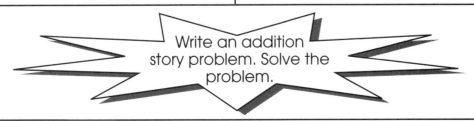

Name

Identifying key subtraction words

Unit 8

There are some key words that tell you to subtract when you solve story problems. They are: *have left, how many more, how many fewer, how much change, difference.*

When subtracting money, it is important to line up the dollar signs in their own column.

Circle the key subtraction words. Then write a problem and find the answer. Be careful! You will need these prices to solve some problems, but not all.

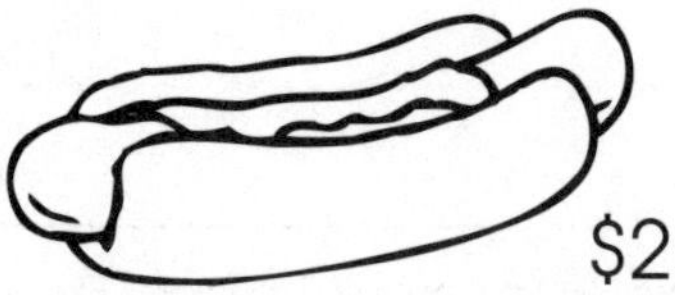

$2.38

$1.29

$1.38

$1.34

Mr. Smith bought a hot dog during the play. He paid with $3.00. How much change will he get? $3.00 − 2.38 = $ .62	A. How much more does popcorn cost than a soda?
B. The class sold 26 sodas and 14 cupcakes. How many fewer cupcakes did they sell?	C. Ms. Green bought 10 sodas and 3 hot dogs. How many more sodas did she buy?
D. What is the difference in price between a hot dog and a soda?	E. Erin bought a soda. She paid with $1.50. How much change will she get?
F. How much more does a cupcake cost than a soda?	G. The class sold 42 bags of popcorn and 18 hot dogs. How many more bags of popcorn did they sell?

Name

Determining necessary information

Unit 8

Sometimes problem solving can be difficult because the story tells you information that you do not need. Do not let unneeded information fool you! Try this:

1. Read the story and the question.
2. Read the question again.
3. Circle the numbers in the story that you need to answer the question.
4. Cross out the number(s) you do not need so they will not confuse you!
5. Watch for key words and answer the question. Label the answer with the story unit.

Use the five steps to find the answers.

A. Ms. Jackson has ⑤ poodles, ⑥ boxers, and ~~4~~ cats. How many dogs does she have in all?	B. Mr. Black has 8 black labs, 4 terriers, and 3 poodles. How many more black labs than terriers does he have?
C. Mr. Zucker has 14 terriers. Eight of them are boys, and 6 are girls. How many more boys than girls are there?	D. Ms. Nimm has 5 black labs, 8 yellow labs, and 3 boxers. How many labs does she have combined?
E. Mr. Kelly has raised beagles for 18 years. He has 12 adults and 28 puppies. How many beagles does he have total?	F. Ms. Miller has 4 dogs. The oldest is 15 years old and the youngest is 3 years old. What is the difference in their ages?
G. Ms. Lee has 3 dogs. They weigh 14 pounds, 11 pounds, and 37 pounds. How much do the dogs weigh combined?	H. Mr. Larry boards dogs. His kennel holds 91 dogs. He has 68 dogs in the kennel now. Fourteen dogs are black labs. How many spaces does he have left?

Name

Using a picture to problem solve

Unit 8

Some types of problem solving are difficult to follow with words. Try using a picture and the story's clues to help you.

Welcome to the dog show! Color the pictures using the clues below.

A. The big dogs are brown, black, and white. The black dog is under the brown dog. The white dog is on top of the brown dog.	B. The ribbons are red, blue, and yellow. The red ribbon is not next to the yellow ribbon. The yellow ribbon is not first.
C. The stages are blue, purple, and red. The purple stage is next to the blue stage. The red stage is not next to the blue stage.	D. The small dogs are brown, black, and white. The brown dog does not have a puffy tail. The black dog has pointed ears.
E. The trophies are red, blue, green, and yellow. The blue trophy is the biggest. The red trophy is not by the blue one, but is by the yellow one. The green trophy is by the red one.	F. The flags are purple, green, blue, and red. The green flag is by the blue one. The red flag is next to the green flag, and the purple flag is next to the red flag.

Name

Illustrating equal groups in word problems **Unit 8**

Another type of problem solving may tell a story that involves equal sets. A key word to watch for is *each*. You may also see the addition key words because multiplying means adding the same number over and over. When you read a story about sets, it may help to draw a picture.

Draw a picture to go with each story. Then count to find the total.

A. You see two beach towels. On each towel, there are four buckets. How many buckets are there in all?

= 8 buckets

B. Six starfish washed up on the sand. Each starfish has five legs. How many legs is that altogether?

= ☐ ______

C. Three children are swimming in the ocean. Each child is wearing two fins. How many fins are there combined?

= ☐ ______

D. Five children are playing in the waves. Each of them has three balls. How many balls are there?

= ☐ ______

E. Three buckets are sitting in the sun. Each bucket has four shovels in it. How many shovels are there in all?

= ☐ ______

F. Seven seashells wash onto the sand. Each shell has an animal living in it. How many animals are there?

= ☐ ______

Name

Writing a multiplication problem to match a story

Unit 8

It may become confusing when you see *in all, altogether, total,* and *combined.* How will you know whether to add or multiply? Think about the story and ask yourself if it involves equal groups. If so, it is a multiplication problem.

Write a problem for each story below. If you are unsure, draw a small picture to help you.

A. We see 3 groups of fish in the water. Each group has 2 fish. How many fish are there in all? ☐ x ☐ = ☐ ______	B. Next, we spot 3 groups of sharks. There are 4 in each group. How many sharks is that altogether? ☐ x ☐ = ☐ ______
C. To the back of our boat we notice 5 groups of dolphins with 3 in each group. How many dolphins did we see? ☐ x ☐ = ☐ ______	D. Later, we come across 4 groups of swordfish. Each group has 4 fish. How many total swordfish? ☐ x ☐ = ☐ ______
E. Soon, we spot 2 groups of rainbow fish. Each group has 5 fish. How many rainbow fish are there combined? ☐ x ☐ = ☐ ______	F. Near sunset, 2 groups with 4 fish in each swim near our boat. How many fish altogether swam by? ☐ x ☐ = ☐ ______
G. We see 5 groups of fish jumping in the air. In each group, there are 5 fish. How many fish are there in all? ☐ x ☐ = ☐ ______	H. At sunset, 4 groups of sailfish swim near our boat. There are 2 fish in each group. How many sailfish do we see? ☐ x ☐ = ☐ ______

Name

Choosing the operation

Unit 8

Use these steps to help you problem solve:

1. Read the story and its question.
2. Read the question again.
3. Circle the numbers in the story that you need to answer the question.
4. Cross out the numbers you do not need. Now they will not confuse you!
5. Watch for key words and equal groups.
6. Choose to +, −, or x.
7. Answer the question.

Use the steps to find the answers.

A. Our family drove 453 miles on vacation. We crossed 4 states. We stopped 2 times in each state. How many times did we stop?

B. We went to an amusement park. There were 4 roller coasters. We rode each one 3 times. How many times did we ride them in all?

C. We hiked 12 miles on Monday. We rode our bikes 23 miles on Tuesday and 31 miles on Wednesday. How far did we ride bikes altogether?

D. We read books while traveling. My sister read 473 pages, and my mom read 394 pages. How many more pages did my sister read than my mom?

E. We stopped at 2 aquariums. There were 356 sharks at one and 358 sharks at the other. How many sharks did we see in all?

F. I wrote about our trip in my journal. I wrote 64 words the first day and 49 words the last day. How many more words did I write the first day?

Name

Unit 8 Test

Page 1

Problem Solving

Read or listen to the question. Fill in the circle beside the best answer.

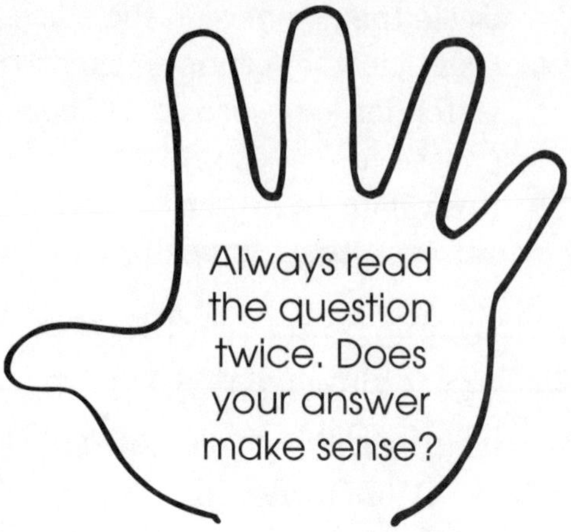
Always read the question twice. Does your answer make sense?

❑ Example:
Four bikes are entered in a 10-mile race. Each bike has 2 wheels. How many wheels are there in all?

8	12	16	14
Ⓐ	Ⓑ	Ⓒ	Ⓓ

Answer: A because 4 groups of 2 = 4 x 2 = 8.

Now try these. You have 25 minutes. Continue until you see STOP.

1. The Bills score 38 points. The Colts score 62 points. How many more points did the Colts score?

100 points	26 points	24 points	90 points
Ⓐ	Ⓑ	Ⓒ	Ⓓ

2. Danny finds 7 tennis balls, 8 footballs, and 13 baseballs. How many more baseballs than tennis balls did he find?

6 baseballs	5 baseballs	15 baseballs	20 baseballs
Ⓐ	Ⓑ	Ⓒ	Ⓓ

3. Michael found 3 birds' nests in the tree outside his window. Each nest had 5 eggs. How many eggs did Michael spot?

8 eggs	2 eggs	15 eggs	12 eggs
Ⓐ	Ⓑ	Ⓒ	Ⓓ

GO ON

Name

Unit 8 Test

Page 2

4. April Fool's Day is almost here! There are 15 days left in February and 31 days in March. How many total days are there until April Fool's Day?

Ⓐ 10 days Ⓑ 15 days Ⓒ 55 days Ⓓ 46 days

5. Drew brought $4.87 to the fair. He spent $3.49 on tickets. How much money does Drew have left?

Ⓐ $8.36 Ⓑ $1.38 Ⓒ $1.78 Ⓓ $1.58

6. Amy has a stamp collection with 47 stamps. She was given a set of 23 stamps. How many stamps does Amy have combined?

Ⓐ 60 stamps Ⓑ 24 stamps Ⓒ 67 stamps Ⓓ 70 stamps

7. Mark the number sentence that matches the story.

At the class pizza party, the boys ate 17 pieces of pizza, and the girls ate 16 pieces. How many pieces of pizza did they eat in all?

Ⓐ 17 – 16 = ☐ Ⓑ 17 > 16 = ☐

Ⓒ 17 + 16 = ☐ Ⓓ 17 x 16 = ☐

8. Mr. Nells raises pigs. He has 64 adults and 26 babies. How many more adults than babies does Mr. Nells have?

Ⓐ 38 adults Ⓑ 90 adults Ⓒ 58 adults Ⓓ 48 adults

GO ON

Name

Unit 8 Test

9. The school playground has 4 slides. There are 3 children playing on each slide. How many children are there altogether?

Ⓐ 7 children	Ⓑ 12 children	Ⓒ 11 children	Ⓓ 1 child

10. The kids in Room 74 have read 83 books at school and 76 books at home. How many books did they read altogether?

Ⓐ 159 books	Ⓑ 168 books	Ⓒ 233 books	Ⓓ 157 books

11. Which picture matches these clues?

The baseball is next to the football.
The hockey puck is on the right.
The football is not in the middle.

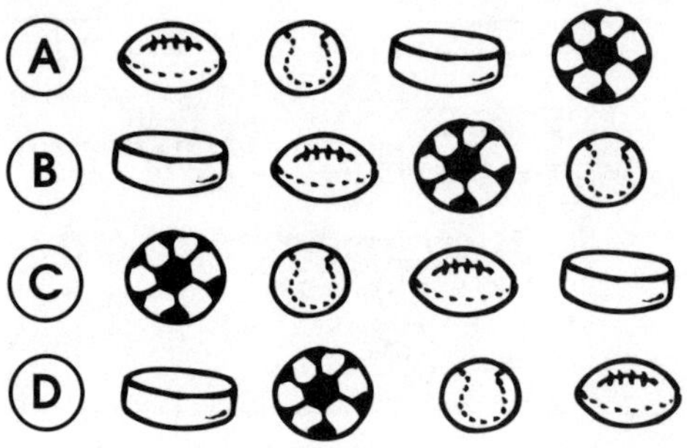

12. Which picture matches the story?

Rachel has 3 bracelets. Each bracelet has 2 beads. How many total beads does Rachel have?

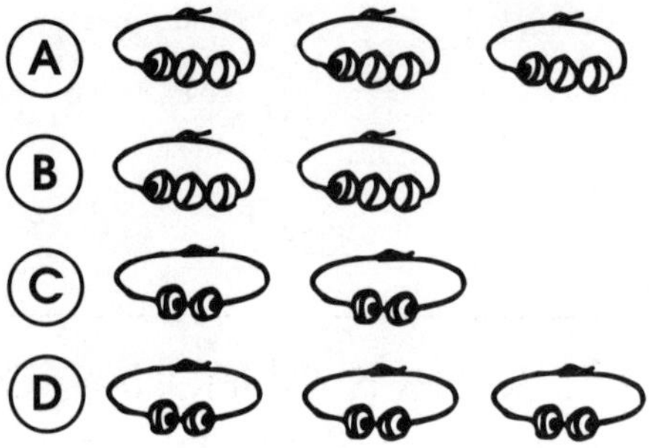

GO ON

Name

Unit 8 Test

13. Find the mystery man by following the clues.

I am wearing a tie, but I am not wearing glasses. I have no curls. Who am I?

Ⓐ Ⓑ Ⓒ Ⓓ

14. Joey earns $2.00 each week. How much total does he earn in 3 weeks?

Ⓐ	Ⓑ	Ⓒ	Ⓓ
$5.00	$6.00	$7.00	$8.00

15. There are two times as many children as there are adults at the party. There are 6 adults. How many children are there?

Ⓐ	Ⓑ	Ⓒ	Ⓓ
12 children	8 children	6 children	18 children

16. Jason is taller than Greg, but shorter than Brooke. Brooke is shorter than Cara. Who is the tallest?

Ⓐ	Ⓑ	Ⓒ	Ⓓ
Jason	Greg	Brooke	Cara

17. Jesse is 42 inches tall. Lynnie is 26 inches tall. How can you find out how much taller Jesse is?

Ⓐ	Ⓑ	Ⓒ	Ⓓ
$42 > 26$	$42 + 26$	$42 - 26$	42×26

GO ON

Name

Unit 8 Test

18. Mark the number sentence that matches the story.

Spot eats 3 times each day. How many times would he eat in 5 days?

Ⓐ $3 \times 5 = \square$ Ⓑ $3 + 5 = \square$

Ⓒ $5 - 3 = \square$ Ⓓ $5 > 3$

19. Mark the problem that matches the story.

Molly walked 5 blocks to the store. She had 74¢. She spent 27¢ on candy. How much does she have left?

Ⓐ 74¢ – 27¢ = ☐ Ⓑ 74¢ + 27¢ = ☐

Ⓒ 5 + 74¢ = ☐ Ⓓ 27¢ – 5 = ☐

20. Al earns 5¢ washing the dishes on Monday. He washes them on Tuesday and Wednesday for the same amount. How much money does Al earn?

25¢	75¢	50¢	15¢
Ⓐ	Ⓑ	Ⓒ	Ⓓ

Write a math story problem. Write a question at the end of the story that includes an addition key word. Solve the problem.

STOP

Name

Final Review Test

Page 1

Read or listen to the question. Use an extra piece of paper to solve the problems. Fill in the circle beside the best answer completely and neatly.

❑ Example:

Find the difference.

$$\begin{array}{r} 819 \\ -\ 477 \\ \hline \end{array}$$

(A) 362 (B) 442

(C) 462 (D) 342

Answer: D because the answer is 342.

Now try these. You have 35 minutes.

Continue until you see STOP.

Remember your Helping Hand Strategies:

1. When using scratch paper, copy carefully.
2. Use your time wisely. If a problem seems tough, skip it and come back to it later.
3. Compare the answer choices. Some answer choices may look very similar.
4. Always read the question twice. Does your answer make sense?

1. Which number will make all of the number sentences true?

$\square + 6 = 15$ $18 - \square = 9$ $17 - 8 = \square$

7	8	9	10
(A)	(B)	(C)	(D)

2. What time is shown?

9:15	4:45	3:45	9:20
(A)	(B)	(C)	(D)

GO ON

Name

Final Review Test

Page 2

3. Which is most likely to be chosen?

Ⓐ 

Ⓑ 

Ⓒ 

Ⓓ 

4. There are 21 children in a class. They have 3 recycling bins. Each bin has 5 pieces of paper. How many pieces of paper are there in all?

24 pieces	15 pieces	8 pieces	16 pieces
Ⓐ	Ⓑ	Ⓒ	Ⓓ

5. One piece of rope is 275 inches long. Another piece is 632 inches long. How long are the ropes combined?

907 in.	897 in.	867 in.	357 in.
Ⓐ	Ⓑ	Ⓒ	Ⓓ

6. A dozen means 12. How many eggs are in 2 dozen? Which number sentence matches the story?

Ⓐ $12 + 2 = 14$ Ⓑ $12 - 2 = 10$

Ⓒ $2 \times 2 = 4$ Ⓓ $12 \times 2 = 24$

GO ON

Name

Final Review Test

7. How many problems equal 8?

2 x 4 = ☐ 16 − 8 = ☐

4 + 4 = ☐ 15 − 6 = ☐

Ⓐ 1 Ⓑ 2

Ⓒ 3 Ⓓ 4

8. You have:

You find a dime.
How much do you have now?

Ⓐ 95¢ Ⓑ 80¢

Ⓒ 85¢ Ⓓ 90¢

9. What part of the group is wearing hats?

Ⓐ $\frac{3}{8}$ Ⓑ $\frac{5}{8}$

Ⓒ $\frac{8}{5}$ Ⓓ $\frac{2}{8}$

10. Joey is older than Becca, but younger than Tara. Tara is younger than Kim. Who is the oldest?

Joey	Becca	Tara	Kim
Ⓐ	Ⓑ	Ⓒ	Ⓓ

11. There are 8 baskets with 4 apples in each. Which number sentence matches the story?

8 + 4 = ☐	8 − 4 = ☐	8 > 4	8 x 4 = ☐
Ⓐ	Ⓑ	Ⓒ	Ⓓ

GO ON

Name

Final Review Test

12. What is the name of this figure?

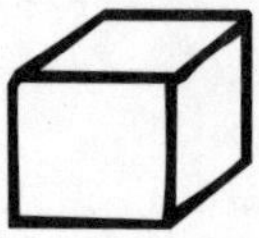

Ⓐ cone Ⓑ cube

Ⓒ sphere Ⓓ pyramid

13. Find the difference.

$$\begin{array}{r} 681 \\ -\ 299 \\ \hline \end{array}$$

382	482	418	392
Ⓐ	Ⓑ	Ⓒ	Ⓓ

14. How much change will you get if you pay with two quarters?

Ⓐ 21¢

Ⓑ 19¢

Ⓒ 23¢

Ⓓ 27¢

15. Which picture shows $\frac{3}{4}$ shaded?

Ⓐ

Ⓑ

Ⓒ

Ⓓ

16. James earned \$5.75 raking leaves. He bought some new markers for \$2.83. How much does he have left?

\$3.12	\$2.92	\$8.58	\$7.12
Ⓐ	Ⓑ	Ⓒ	Ⓓ

17.

$$\begin{array}{r} 819 \\ -\ 477 \\ \hline \end{array}$$

342	482	382	242
Ⓐ	Ⓑ	Ⓒ	Ⓓ

GO ON

Name

Final Review Test

18. Which object weighs less than 2 pounds?

 Ⓐ

 Ⓑ

 Ⓒ

 Ⓓ

19. Which of these can be folded in half so that both sides are exactly the same?

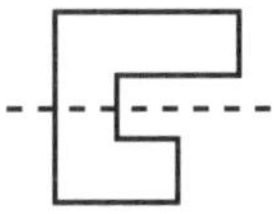 Ⓐ

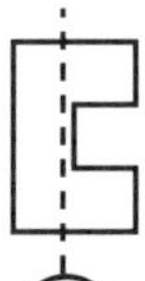 Ⓑ

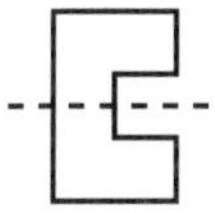 Ⓒ

 Ⓓ

20. You had $2.00 to pay for popcorn. This is the change you got:

How much did the popcorn cost?

Ⓐ	Ⓑ	Ⓒ	Ⓓ
$1.00	$1.50	$1.75	$2.50

21. Which clock shows quarter after 8:00?

 Ⓐ

 Ⓑ

 Ⓒ

 Ⓓ

22. The parade started at 2:00. It ended at 4:00. How long did the parade last?

Start

End

Ⓐ 1 hour

Ⓑ 1 ½ hours

Ⓒ 2 hours

Ⓓ 2 ½ hours

GO ON

Name

Final Review Test

Page 6

Use the graph to answer questions 23 and 24.

Our Class Lunches

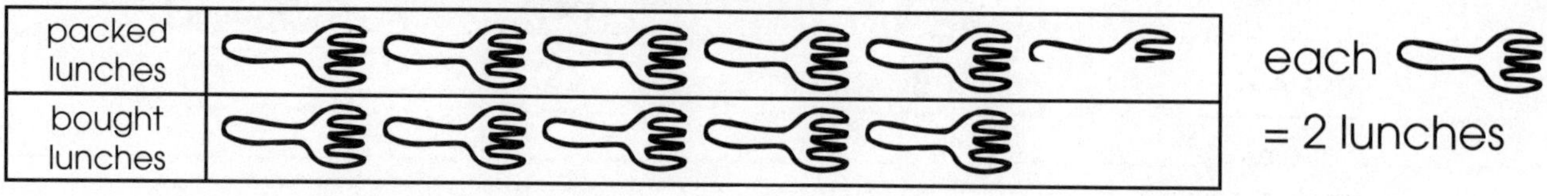

23. How many more children packed their lunches than bought their lunches at school?

4	2	3	1
(A)	(B)	(C)	(D)

24. How many total children are in the class?

21	19	10	12
(A)	(B)	(C)	(D)

25.

$$\begin{array}{r} 754 \\ -\ 508 \\ \hline \end{array}$$

346	246	256	344
(A)	(B)	(C)	(D)

26. Which number can be rounded to 500?

575	416	566	474
(A)	(B)	(C)	(D)

27. Which number sentence matches the story?

Alex has sold 54 boxes of cookies and 79 boxes of candy. How many boxes of cookies and candy has he sold altogether?

(A) 79 – 54 = _____

(B) 54 + 79 = _____

(C) 54 < 79 = _____

(D) 54 x 79 = _____

GO ON

Name

Final Review Test

Page 7

Use the tally chart to answer questions 28 and 29.

Transportation in Our City

	Men	Women	Children
Bus	𝍸 𝍸 ||||	𝍸 ||||	𝍸 ||
Train	𝍸 𝍸	𝍸 |||	𝍸 𝍸 |

28. How many people rode the train?

24 Ⓐ 18 Ⓑ 25 Ⓒ 29 Ⓓ

29. How many more men than women rode the bus?

5 Ⓐ 7 Ⓑ 9 Ⓒ 11 Ⓓ

30.

$$\begin{array}{r} 658 \\ -\ 273 \\ \hline \end{array}$$

385 Ⓐ 831 Ⓑ 821 Ⓒ 931 Ⓓ

Jamir is going to buy a snow cone for 75¢. Show four ways he could pay the exact amount. Label the coins:

P = penny
N = nickel
Q = quarter
D = dime

STOP

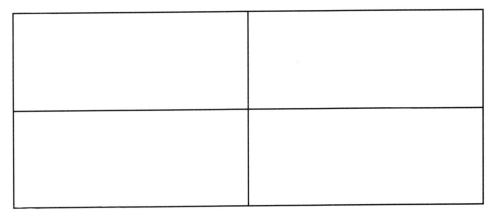

Answer Key

Page 5

A. 48; B. 26; C. 45; D. 66; E. 73

Page 6

A. 60 + 7 =67; B. 50 + 0 = 50; C. 90 + 3 = 93; D. 70 + 8 = 78

Page 7

Bottom car wins.

Page 8

1	2	3	4	5	6	7	8	9	10
11	12	13	14	15	16	17	18	19	20
21	22	23	24	25	26	27	28	29	30
31	32	33	34	35	36	37	38	39	40
41	42	43	44	45	46	47	48	49	50
51	52	53	54	55	56	57	58	59	60
61	62	63	64	65	66	67	68	69	70
71	72	73	74	75	76	77	78	79	80
81	82	83	84	85	86	87	88	89	90
91	92	93	94	95	96	97	98	99	100

Page 9

1, 21, 23, 26, 31, 35, 40, 42, 46, 49; 51, 60, 71, 78, 81, 84, 89, 90, 93, 99

Page 10

A. 46 + 10 = 56; B. 63 + 10 = 73; C. 70 + 10 = 80; D. 57 + 10 = 67; E. 79 + 10 = 89; F. 58; G. 45; H. 17; I. 82; J. 18; K. 94; L. 26; M. 69; N. 73

Page 11

A. 36; B. 65; C. 58; D. 80; E. 48; F. 36, 2, 64; 55, 18, 73, 27

Page 12

Numbers ending in 5 should be colored yellow. Numbers ending in 0 should be colored yellow and red. A. 20, 25; B. 50, 60, 100; C. 80, 85, 90, 100; D. 20, 30, 40, 50; E. 35, 40, 55, 60, 65

Page 13

A. 2, 4, 6, 8, 10, 12, 14, 16, 18, 20, 22, 24, 26, 28, 30, 32, 34, 36, 38, 40; B. 3, 6, 9, 12, 15, 18, 21, 24, 27, 30, 33, 36, 39; C. 15, 21; D. 20, 24; E. 8, 14; F. 3, 12; G. 4, 6, 12; H. 3, 12, 15

Unit 1 Test

1. A; 2. D; 3. C; 4. B; 5. A; 6. C; 7. A; 8. C; 9. C; 10. D; 11. D; 12. B; 13. D; 14. C; 15. A; 16. B; 17. C; 18. A; 19. C; 20. A; Constructed-response answers will vary.

Page 19

A. 226; B. 156; C. 118; D. 213; E. 164

Page 20

A. 500 + 60 + 8 = 568; B. 900 + 0 + 7 = 907; C. 300 + 80 = 2 = 382; D. 800 + 30 + 6 = 836; E. 700 + 60 + 4 = 764

Page 21

HE WAS IN SHOCK!

Page 22

A. 435; B. 768; C. 910; D. 378; E. 387; F. 199; G. 136; H. 683; I. 614; J. 815; K. 136, 199, 378, 387, 435, 614, 683, 768, 815, 910

Page 23

A. 981; B. 963; C. 705; D. 712; E. 762; F. 514; G. 330; H. 189; I. 378

Page 24

A. fourth; B. fifth; C. ninth; D. second; E. first; F. sixth; G. third; 8. seventh; I. eighth

Page 25

Page 26

A. 60¢; B. 70¢; C. 80¢; D. 90¢; E. 60¢; F. 20¢; G. 40¢; H. 40¢; I. 20¢; J. 50¢; K. 90¢; L. 80¢; M. 30¢; N. 10¢; O. 70¢; P. 80

Page 27

258	↑	300
722	↓	700
648	↓	600
391	↑	400
928	↓	900
453	↑	500
137	↓	100
558	↑	600

902	↓	900
445	↓	400
584	↑	600
231	↓	200
616	↓	600
760	↑	800
329	↓	300
870	↑	900

Page 28

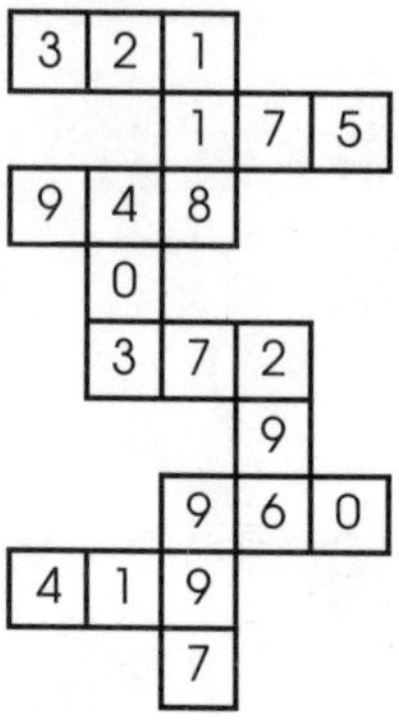

Unit 2 Test

1. B; 2. D; 3. D; 4. C; 5. A; 6. C; 7. B; 8. A; 9. B; 10. D; 11. C; 12. A; 13. B; 14. A; 15. D; 16. C; 17. A; 18. C; 19. D; 20. B; Constructed-response answers will vary.

Page 34

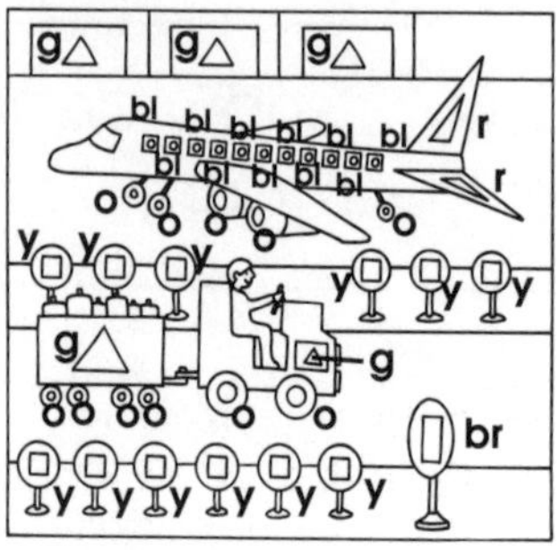

Page 35

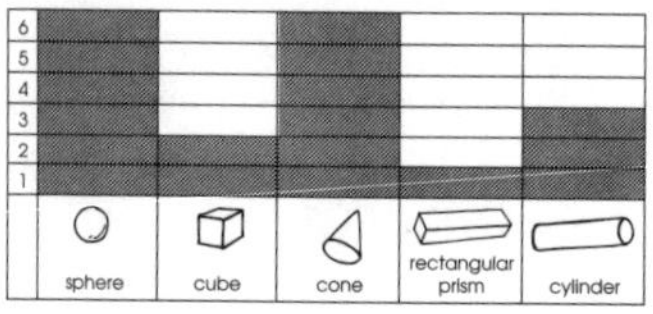

Page 36

Shape	Draw the figure.	# Points	# Sides	# corner angles
A. square	□	4	4	4
B. rectangle	▯	4	4	4
C. diamond	◇	4	4	4
D. octagon		8	8	8
E. triangle	△	3	3	3

Page 37

Page 38

1. B; 2. B; 3. A; 4. C

Page 39

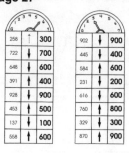

Page 40

A. head = 5 + 5 + 5 + 5 = 20 units; body = 9 + 12 + 9 + 12 = 42 units; ear = 2 + 2 + 2= 6 units; ear = 2 + 2 + 2= 6 units; tail = 2 + 6 + 4 + 3 + 2 + 5 + 4 + 4 = 30 units; B. head = 20 units; ears = 12 units; body = 44 units; tail = 26 units; front leg = 18 units; back leg = 13 units

Answer Key

Page 41

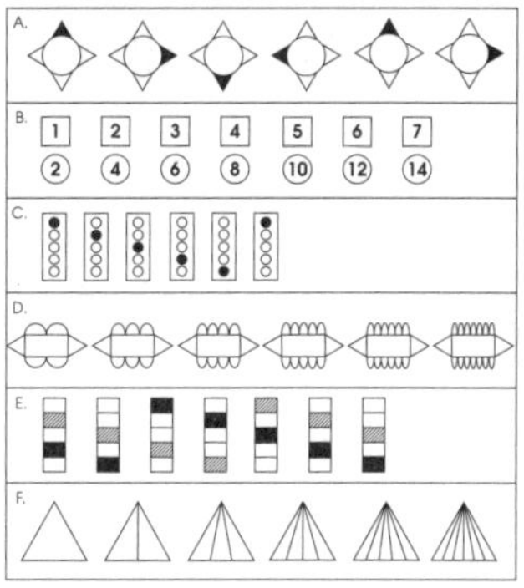

Unit 3 Test

1. D; 2. A; 3. A; 4. C; 5. B; 6. C; 7. A; 8. D; 9. D; 10. A; 11. A; 12. B; 13. A; 14. B; 15. D; 16. B; 17. C; 18. C; 19. B; 20. A; Constructed-response answers will vary.

Page 47

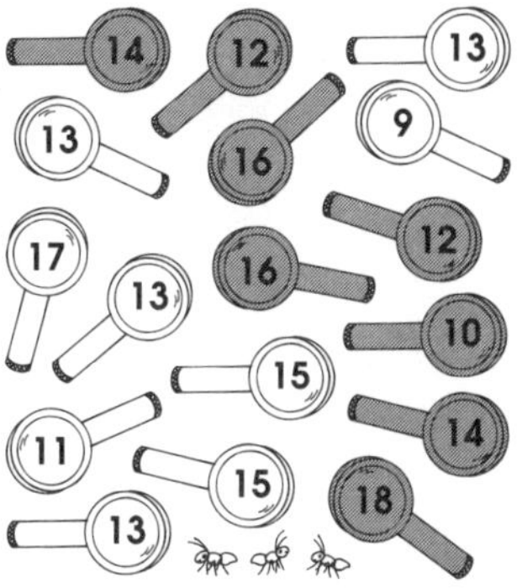

Page 48

A. 4, 7, 8, 5, 6, 8; B. 8, 9, 7, 6, 6, 3; C. 5, 9, 6, 9, 5, 8; D. 7, 9, 9, 7

Page 49

A. 538, 982, 834, 737; B. 646, 729, 996; C. 886, 683, 934, 475; The bank on the left is the winner.

Page 50

A. 79 > 77; B. 599 > 525; C. 185 < 747; D. 657 < 976; E. 819 < 893; F. 799 > 762; G. 89 > 80; H. 499 < 587; I. 827 > 787

Page 51

A. 43; B. 68; C. 91; D. 89; E. 70; F. 31; G. 80; H. 28; I. 74; J. 69; K. 93

Page 52

A. 82, 91, 71, 92; B. 71, 75, 42, 42; C. 70, 90, 94, 88; D. 91, 63, 94, 76

Page 53

MARBLE CAKE!

Page 54

A. 945, 538, 513, 829; B. 478, 809, 937, 707; C. 288, 859, 640, 654

Page 55

A. 920, 721, 752, 920; B. 933, 403, 821, 956; C. 862, 911, 816, 742; D. 652, 633, 732, 902

Page 56

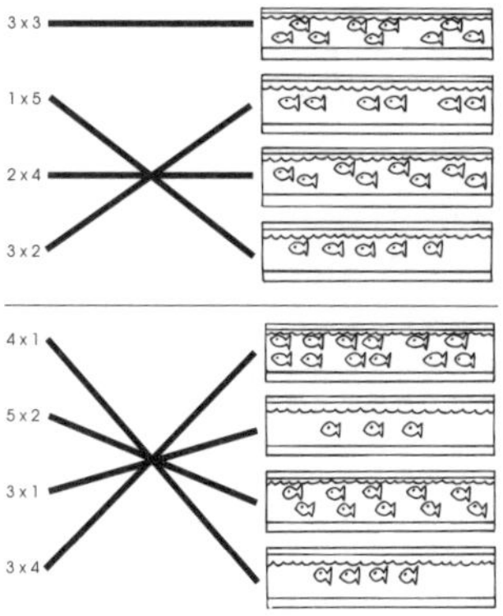

Page 57

A. 8; B. 9; C. 12; D. 12; E. 4; F. 10; G. 4; Check students' drawings.

Unit 4 Test

1. C; 2. B; 3. A; 4. D; 5. C; 6. B; 7. D; 8. A; 9. C; 10. C; 11. D; 12. A; 13. B; 14. B; 15. C; 16. A; 17. B; 18. D; 19. B; 20. A; Constructed-response answers will vary.

Midway Review Test

1. D; 2. B; 3. D; 4. C; 5. B; 6. C; 7. A; 8. B; 9. B; 10. C; 11. C; 12. B; 13. A; 14. C; 15. B; 16. A; 17. D; 18. B; 19. C; 20. B; Constructed-response answers will vary.

Page 67

A. 5, 6, 3; B. 8, 7, 4; C. 3, 7, 4; D. 8, 5, 4; E. 9, 6, 9

The bottom super hero will fly the fastest.

Page 68

A. 7, 6, 8, 9; B. 7, 9, 8, 6; C. 3, 5, 7, 8; D. 2, 5, 6, 9; E. 6, 9, 7, 8; F. 3, 7, 8, 4; G. 9, 5, 6, 8, 7; H. 9, 4, 7, 6, 8, 5

Page 69

A. 7; B. 6; C. 3; D. 5; E. 9; F. 4; Moore, Smith, Jones, Hall, Nelson, Miller

Page 70

A. 242, 317, 733, 311; B. 720, 401, 514, 201; C. 335, 1, 110, 453

Page 71

A. 2 tens, 14 ones; B. 5 tens, 18 ones; 6 tens, 12 ones; 4 tens, 14 ones; C. 8 tens, 16 ones; 5 tens, 10 ones; 7 tens, 14 ones; D. 6 tens, 10 ones; 7 tens, 17 ones; 0 tens, 16 ones; E. 0 tens, 12 ones; 1 ten, 10 ones; 3 tens, 13 ones

Page 72

A. 46, 36, 58, 7; B. 11, 19, 28, 77; C. 14, 48, 16, 69

Page 73

A. 113, 329, 425; B. 317, 319, 743; C. 122, 233, 545; D. 357, 209, 347

Page 74

A. 192, 241, 190, 89; B. 881, 563, 91, 365; C. 356, 433, 452, 173

Page 75

THE PLYMOUTH ROCK!

Page 76

A. 900 – 300 = 600; B. 700 – 200 = 500; C. 900 – 400 = 500; D. 300 – 200 = 100; E. 400 – 400 = 0; F. 600 – 200 = 400; G. 800 – 200 = 600; H. 800 – 500 = 300

Unit 5 Test

1. B; 2. D; 3. C; 4. A; 5. B; 6. C; 7. C; 8. A; 9. D; 10. A; 11. B; 12. C; 13. C; 14. B; 15. A; 16. C; 17. A; 18. D; 19. B; 20. C; Constructed-response answers will vary.

Page 81

A. 67¢; B. 83¢; C. 98¢; D. 81¢; E. 68¢; F. 36¢

Page 82

A. 91¢ – 34¢ = 57¢; B. 61¢ – 29¢ = 32¢; C. 90¢ – 52¢ = 38¢; D. 79¢ – 23¢ = 56¢

Page 83

A. 3:00; B. 7:15; C. 12:45; D. 2:25; E. 8:10; F. 10:30; G. 6:30; H. 5:20

Page 84

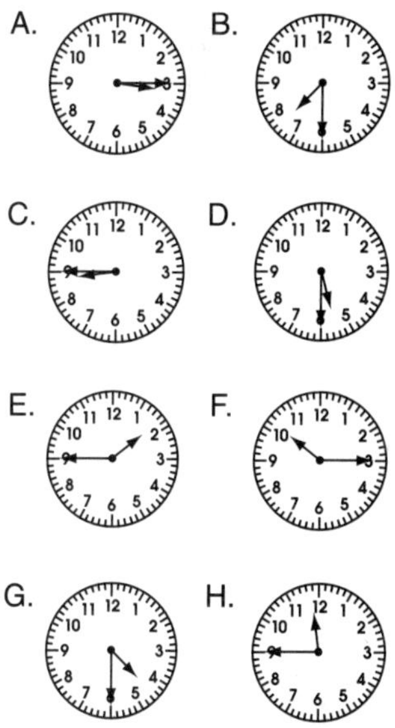

Page 85

A. 30 minutes; B. 7:40; C. 1 hour 30 minutes; D. 6:20; E. 25 minutes; F. 9:55

Page 86

A. 4; B. Sunday; C. 30; D. June 21; E. June 3; F. 5

Page 87

A. 5 pounds; B. 3 gallons; C. 80° F; D. 10 inches; E. 18 inches; F. 30° F; G. 2 liters; H. 15 kilograms

Answer Key

Page 88

Iggy: 4, 7, 3, 1, 15; Slinky: 5, 13, 11, 8, 37

Unit 6 Test

1. B; 2. A; 3. B; 4. C; 5. B; 6. A; 7. C; 8. B; 9. B; 10. B; 11. D; 12. A; 13. B; 14. C; 15. C; 16. A; 17. B; 18. C; 19. D; 20. A; Constructed-response answers will vary.

Page 95

A. 

B. 

Page 96

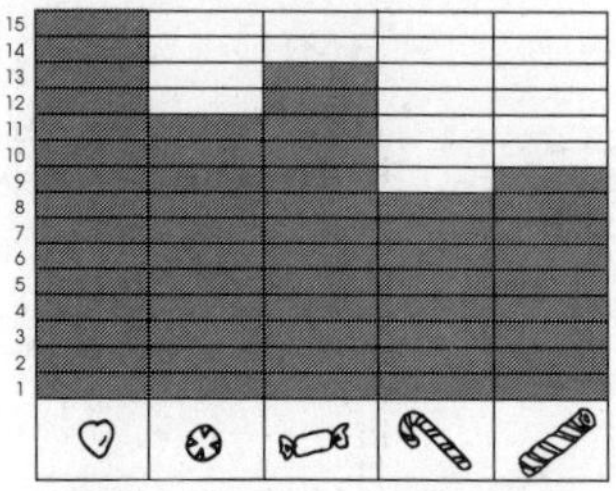

A. ; B. ; C. 5; D. 17; E. ; F. 6; G. 32

Page 97

A. 15; B. 21; C. Princess; D. 19; E. Queen; F. 4; G. 35; H. Prince

Page 98

A. 17; B. 13; C. King Ludwig; D. 61; E. King Johans; F. King Johans; G. King Johans

Page 99

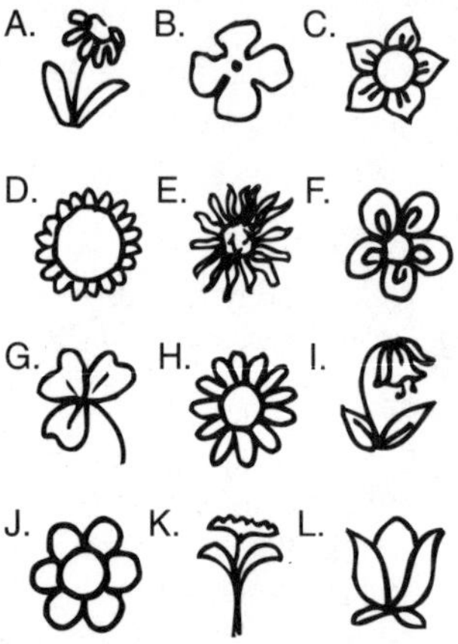

Page 100

A. 8; B. 15; C. apple; D. 7; E. 33; F. celery; G. 7; H. 32

Page 101

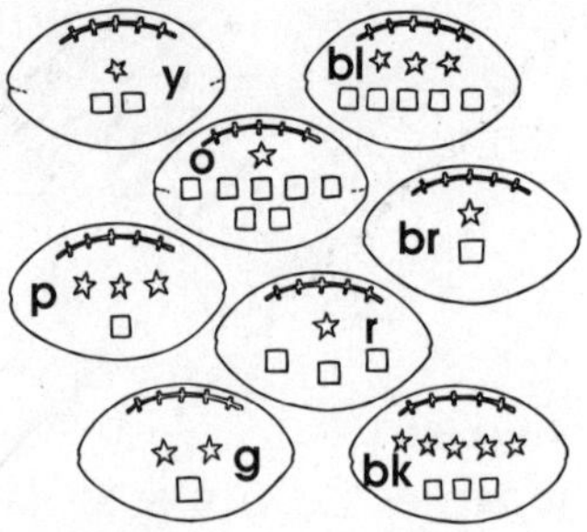

Page 102

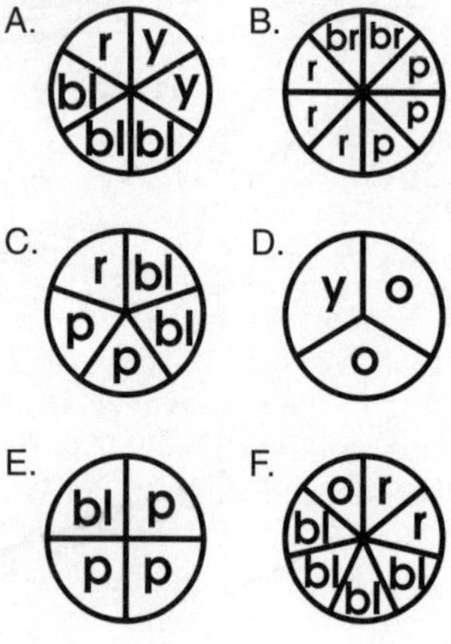

Unit 7 Test

1. B; 2. D; 3. C; 4. D; 5. A; 6. D; 7. A; 8. A; 9. D; 10. C; 11. A; 12. B; 13. B; 14. D; 15. B; 16. C; 17. D; 18. B; 19. B; 20. A; Constructed-response graphs will vary.

Page 107

A. total, 49 children;
B. altogether, 19 parents;
C. combined, 200 tickets;
D. in all, 5 shows;
E. combined, 69 props

Page 108

A. How much more, $.09;
B. How many fewer, 12;
C. How many more, 7;
D. difference, $1.09; E. How much change, $.21; F. How much more, $.05; G. How many more, 24

Page 109

A. 4 cats, 11 dogs; B. 3 poodles, 4 black labs; C. 14 terriers, 2 boys; D. 3 boxers, 13 labs; E. 18 years, 40 beagles; F. 4 dogs, 12 years; G. 3 dogs, 62 pounds; H. 14 black labs, 23 spaces

Page 110

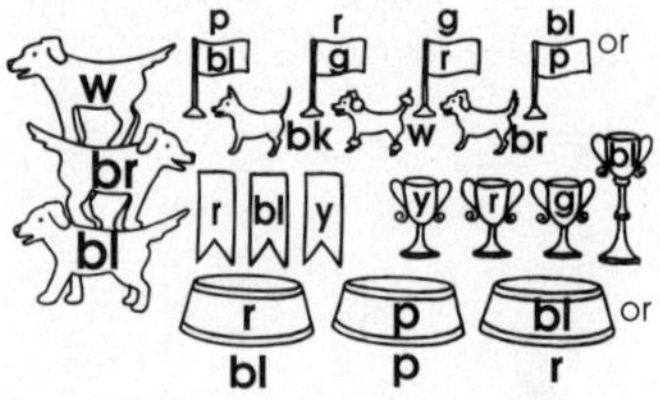

Page 111

A. 2x4=8 buckets; B. 6x5=30 legs; C. 3x2=6 fins; D. 5x3=15 balls; E. 3x4=12 shovels; F. 7x1=7 animals

Page 112

A. 3 x 2 = 6 fish; B. 3 x 4 = 12 sharks; C. 5 x 3 = 15 dolphins; D. 4 x 4 = 16 swordfish; E. 2 x 5 = 10 rainbow fish; F. 2 x 4 = 8 fish; G. 5 x 5 = 25 fish; H. 4 x 2 = 8 sailfish

Page 113

A. 4 x 2 = 8 times; B. 4 x 3 = 12 times; C. 23 + 31 = 54 miles; D. 473 – 394 = 79 pages; E. 356 + 358 = 714 sharks; F. 64 – 49 = 15 words

Unit 8 Test

1. C; 2. A; 3. C; 4. D; 5. B; 6. D; 7. C; 8. A; 9. B; 10. A; 11. A; 12. D; 13. C; 14. B; 15. A; 16. D; 17. C; 18. A; 19. A; 20. D; Constructed-response answers will vary.

Final Review Test

1. C; 2. C; 3. B; 4. B; 5. A; 6. D; 7. C; 8. C; 9. B; 10. D; 11. D; 12.B; 13. A; 14. A; 15. A; 16. B; 17. A; 18. A; 19.C; 20. C; 21. D; 22. C; 23. D; 24. A; 25. B; 26. D; 27. B; 28. D; 29. A; 30. A; Constructed-response answers will vary.